# Street Cred

# Street Cred
Local banks and strong local economies

Stephen L. Clarke

Civitas: Institute for the Study of Civil Society
London

First Published April 2012

© Civitas 2012
55 Tufton Street
London SW1P 3QL

email: books@civitas.org.uk

All rights reserved

ISBN 978-1-906837-39-6

Independence: Civitas: Institute for the Study of Civil Society is a registered educational charity (No. 1085494) and a company limited by guarantee (No. 04023541). Civitas is financed from a variety of private sources to avoid over-reliance on any single or small group of donors.

All publications are independently refereed. All the Institute's publications seek to further its objective of promoting the advancement of learning. The views expressed are those of the authors, not of the Institute.

Typeset by
Kevin Dodd

Printed in Great Britain by
Berforts Group Ltd
Stevenage, SG1 2BH

# Contents

|  | *Page* |
|---|---|
| **Tables** | vii |
| **The author** | viii |
| **Acknowledgements** | viii |
| **Foreword** | ix |
| **Summary** | xii |
| **Preface** | xiv |

**1. The British banking market** — 1
  The British banking oligopoly — 2
  Failing to serve British businesses — 2
  Failing consumers — 7
  The opportunities for new banks — 8

**2. Swiss Cantonal banks** — 11
  Serving the Swiss economy — 11
  The constitution of the Swiss Cantonal banks — 13
  Success and stability — 15

**3. The German Sparkassen** — 19
  Serving the German economy — 19
  The constitution of the Sparkassen — 22
  Credit Guarantees — 24
  Resilient and profitable — 26

**4. Trustee Savings Banks** — 29
  The origins and constitution of the Trustee Savings Banks — 29
  Trustee Savings Banks and local economies — 32
  Government mishandling and the 'privatisation' of the Trustee Savings Banks — 35

| | |
|---|---|
| 5. **Localised banking today: The Airdrie Savings Bank and Handelsbanken** | 39 |
| The origins and constitution of the Airdrie Savings Bank | 39 |
| Small but successful | 40 |
| Handelsbanken: A Swedish relationship bank in Britain | 43 |
| 6. **The barriers to British local banks** | 46 |
| Completing the FSA application | 47 |
| Achieving regulatory approval | 48 |
| Meeting capital requirements | 49 |
| Meeting liquidity requirements | 50 |
| Accessing the payment systems | 52 |
| Increasing market share | 53 |
| Regulating diversity | 54 |
| 7. **Conclusion: British local banks** | 57 |
| Removing the barriers to entry in banking | 57 |
| Creating a legal structure for local banks | 59 |
| Encouraging the growth of local banks | 62 |
| Local authorities and local banks | 63 |
| Local banks and other financial institutions | 66 |
| **Notes** | 69 |

## Tables

*Page*

Table 1: Lending to businesses (which includes manufacturing and service firms), lending for property (which includes personal mortgages, loans to the construction and real estate sectors) and lending to financial firms (which includes financial intermediation firms and insurance firms) between 2000 and 2010. (£ millions) — 3

Table 2: Selected assets and liabilities of the Cantonal Banks and Large Commercial Banks in Switzerland (CHF billions) — 11

Table 3: Excess capital of the Cantonal Banks and Large Commercial Banks as a percentage of the required capital — 16

Table 4: Savings and deposits and mortgages of the Cantonal Banks and Large Commercial Banks (CHF billions) — 16

Table 5: Credit provided by Swiss banks (excluding mortgage credit) (CHF billions) — 17

Table 6: Profit and loss account of the Cantonal Banks and the Large Commercial Banks (CHF millions) — 18

Table 7: Assets and Liabilities of the Large Commercial Banks and the Sparkassen — 19

Table 8: Lending to different industries by the Sparkassen and Large Commercial Banks (as a percentage of total lending) — 20

Table 9: Lending volumes during the financial crisis by the Sparkassen and Large Commercial Banks (€ billions) — 26

Table 10: Profit for the financial year after tax as a percentage of the average capital as shown on the balance sheet — 27

Table 11: Sums to depositors in the Special Investment Departments (£ sterling) (not adjusted for inflation) — 34

Table 12: Airdrie Savings Bank five year financial summary (£ thousands) — 42

Table 13: Capital ratio of the Handelsbanken group and lending volumes in the UK (£ millions) — 44

# The author

Stephen Clarke studied Modern History and Politics at St Anne's College, Oxford University. He is currently a Research Fellow at Civitas examining the state of the UK economy and its financial services. In November last year he wrote 'German savings banks and Swiss cantonal banks, lessons for the UK', which highlighted the benefits that local banks could bring to the British economy. His other publications include 'Four Industries and a Funeral? Import Substitutions – a Test of the Possibilities in the Glass, Paper, Steel and Automotive Sectors' and 'The STEM subject push'.

# Acknowledgements

I would like to thank Jim Lindsay, Chief Executive Officer of the Airdrie Savings Bank and Wolfgang Neumann, EU Representative of the Sparkassen-Finanzgruppe, for their assistance and for checking that I had not made any errors in describing the success of their banks. I would also like to thank Dirk Bennett, a family friend who provided invaluable translations of the German Länder constitutions that allowed me fully to understand their unique structure. A number of individuals who are planning on launching new banks and those with experience of setting up banks also helped me, although they wish to remain anonymous. It is safe to say that without their help the almost byzantine system that new entrants need to navigate would have remained a mystery to me. Thanks are due to Tony Greenham, Head of Finance and Business at the New Economics Foundation, for his comments and suggestions. Finally I must acknowledge the assistance of everyone at Civitas, in particular Lucy Hatton, who helped to comb out the errors. Any that remain are purely my own.

# *Foreword*

The shortage of finance for small and medium-sized businesses (SMEs) has been a problem for several decades. As long ago as 1931 the Macmillan committee identified a gap in the availability of investment funds for SMEs and similar complaints continue to the present day.

In 2010 Civitas published an online report showing how two of Europe's most successful economies, Germany and Switzerland, had overcome the problem. German savings banks (Sparkassen) hold about one-third of that country's bank assets and play a vital role in funding German industry. Swiss cantonal banks are proportionately smaller but play a pivotal role in their respective cantons. *Street Cred*, by Stephen Clarke, extends and deepens the 2010 report.

Three main characteristics of local German banks stand out. First, like many German organisations there is a dual-board structure, a supervisory board and an executive. Two-thirds of the members of the supervisory board are nominated by the local authority and one-third by the employees. Second, party-political abuse of power is discouraged by requiring the executive board to run the bank on commercial lines. The Sparkassen are regulated by the same laws as all other banks, although they face some additional obligations. Third, loans can only be made within a defined local authority area. This local focus means that bank staff are familiar with local businesses and able to judge more effectively the reliability of applicants for loans.

Does it lead to wasteful lending? Banks will lend if there is a potentially high return or if there is collateral. Lending for domestic mortgages or commercial property is more attractive for banks because there is both a potential cash flow and collateral if things go wrong. SMEs are at a disadvantage because they often have no collateral. In such cases banks frequently require personal guarantees from directors, perhaps by putting a charge on their domestic residence. The upshot is that many creditworthy small businesses are unable to obtain funding.

In Germany, however, the absence of collateral is overcome by a system of guarantees and risk-spreading. The funds available to local German banks for lending are primarily customer deposits, which must be safeguarded. Consequently, German local banks are part of a national system that spreads risk across a system of regional banks and national institutions. In addition, Germany also has credit guarantee banks. They are non-profit associations of lenders that historically provided sureties worth 80% of the loan value. Typically a guarantee bank takes up to 35% of the risk, while the federal government takes 40% and the region 25%. The borrower pays an initial fee of 1-1.5% of the loan plus an annual commission of up to 1.5% of the amount outstanding each year. During the recent downturn, guarantees were increased to 90% of the loan value.

These locally rooted institutions gave Germany a tremendous advantage after the financial crash of September 2008. The German people had under their direct control institutions with the power to react spontaneously to the crash. If a local firm was in trouble, the neighbourhood bank could help and usually did. Local businesses were not at the mercy of the big commercial banks. Local banks increased lending to business during the recent downturn. From 2006 to 2011 lending increased by 17%, whereas German commercial banks reduced lending by nearly 10%. Local banks also lent more in total than commercial banks: in July 2008 they lent €290 billion and commercial banks nearly €200 billion. In 2011 local banks lent €320 billion and commercial banks nearly €180 billion.

The report argues that we should create the legal framework for similar local banks to emerge in the UK. It does not argue that the Government should set up the proposed banks, only that it should create the possibility that they could be established where they are wanted. Nor is it necessary for the new banks to be public-sector bodies. The Localism Act 2011 provides a framework that permits them to take that form, but a variety of other legal structures should also be available, including mutuals, co-ops, private limited companies, community interest companies and trusts.

Local authority involvement has the advantage that councils have the power to take deposits without permission from the regulatory authorities. Moreover, the presence of a supervisory board keeping a watchful eye on the executive board is a useful constraint, although it need not be made up of a mixture of local authority nominees and employees. It could comprise customers in the manner of a consumer co-op; or its members could be trustees, who are charged with safeguarding the social objectives of the bank but barred from profiting personally. More than one approach could work, but the vital insight of the great economist, Hayek, was that the knowledge and understanding that allow us all to make our unique contribution to the advance of civilisation is unavoidably dispersed.

Empowered local institutions create new opportunities for the exercise of personal responsibility by people with personal commitment and distinctive know-how that is invisible to centralised wielders of power, whether in Whitehall or in our huge international banks.

*David G. Green*

# *Summary*

- In September 2011 the Independent Commission on Banking (ICB) released its final report. Although the report was praised for its attempt to improve the stability of the British banking sector, it was widely felt that it failed to address the issue of competition, and did not even touch upon how banks should better serve the British economy.

- The British banking market is one of the least competitive in the developed world. Since the financial crisis there have been 14 mergers in the banking sector. The lack of effective competition in the British banking market is not just the result of there being few large banks, but also a lack of variety amongst banks.

- The lack of competition has a particularly negative effect upon British businesses, especially SMEs that rely on bank loans for investment. The SME market is one of the most concentrated and since the financial crisis SMEs have been starved of credit by the big banks more concerned with repairing their balance sheets.

- More competition is required, but also competition by different banks. Britain does not have a large local bank sector despite being the first country to officially recognise local savings banks in the early 19th century.

- To appreciate the benefits that local banks could bring to the country and the British economy one only has to look at the success of the Swiss Cantonal banks and German Sparkassen that increased lending to businesses after the financial crash in 2008.

- Up until 1986 the Trustee Savings Banks offered some of the services provided by the German Sparkassen and Swiss Cantonal banks. The Trustee Savings Banks illustrate how a network of local banks could develop in Britain today.

- Although the Trustee Savings Banks were controversially privatised in 1986, one bank, the Airdrie Savings Bank, avoided privatisation and has been serving customers in the central belt of Scotland for over twenty years, turning local savings into productive investments. It increased its lending during the financial crisis and has recently expanded its operations. Its success illustrates how a conservative business model can flourish in the modern British banking market.

- Handelsbanken is a commercial Swedish Bank that embraced local banking in the 1970s. It is one of the largest banks in Scandinavia and has opened 57 new branches in the UK since the beginning of 2009. It is another example of how local banks can be profitable and successful in Britain.

- If the Government wants more local banks to emerge then it must remove the significant barriers to entry in the banking market.

- The FSA does little to promote competition and favours applications from 'known' executives. The regulator also penalises online or telephone-only institutions and does not have the necessary resources to efficiently process applications from prospective banks.

- The Government needs to reform the payments system, the capital and liquidity rules and the regulator itself to ensure that new banks can enter the market. Without reform there is little hope that the British banking market can benefit from variety and competition.

- Along with removing the barriers to entry the Government needs to encourage greater diversity in the market. It should create a new legal framework for local banks based on the governance systems of the Sparkassen, Cantonal and Airdrie Savings Bank. Organisations or individuals interested in making use of the framework should be given the necessary assistance to do so.

- Local authorities, recently empowered by the new Localism Act, should be encouraged to set up local banks if there is an unmet demand for banking services in their local community. The Government should assist by publicly funding a number of local banks selected through a competitive tendering process. Surplus capital from the Regional Growth Fund could be used for this.

# *Preface*

In 2010 Civitas published *German savings banks and Swiss Cantonal banks, lessons for the UK*, which described the success of the German Sparkassen (savings banks) and the Swiss Cantonal banks in supporting the real economy, especially small and medium-sized enterprises (SMEs).[1]

This more detailed report takes a closer look at these institutions, along with a number of similar British and foreign banks and updates the argument in the wake of the Vickers report on banking. The report describes how the Government could open up the banking market to more competition, thus permitting locally-oriented banks to emerge and flourish.

# 1. The British banking market

The view, predominant until the recent crisis, that the British financial system was the envy of the world and was serving the domestic economy as well as it served international customers, has been dispelled. Policy makers, the public and many of those in the industry, realise that Britain's financial system needs to reapply itself to the task of channelling savings and investment into productive British businesses. Unfortunately Britain's current crop of banks is unable to do this. The Government must remove the barriers to entry in the banking market and encourage new entrants that can.

Any reform of the banking system will have to address two pivotal issues. The first is the danger that another financial crisis will result from undue risks taken by Britain's large banking sector. The second is the failure of the current system to serve the real economy, consumers and businesses.

The first issue, stability, was investigated by the Independent Commission on Banking (ICB). Its proposals, released in September 2011, focus on ensuring that the commercial and retail arms of Britain's universal banks are not threatened by risks taken by the investment arms of such institutions. Unfortunately the second issue, effectiveness and competition, was barely touched upon by the ICB. The Centre for the Study of Financial Innovation (CSFI) collated 37 responses to the ICB report by academics, financiers and other experts. Eighteen, or nearly 50 per cent, of the respondents explicitly identified competition as an important issue that the ICB's proposals did not substantially deal with. Only two respondents argued that competition in the sector did not need to be improved and, unsurprisingly, these responses came from Sir Win Bischoff, Chairman of Lloyds Banking Group and Angela Knight, Chief Executive of the British Bankers' Association. The CSFI summed up the general feeling that: 'The absence of a blueprint for competition is a criticism voiced by both supporters and detractors'.[2] This is worrying because the British economy needs more than just stable banks, it needs institutions that effectively channel savings and investments into productive enterprises.

## The British banking oligopoly

There have long been concerns about the state of Britain's banking industry. In 2000 Sir Donald Cruickshank, in a report for the Treasury, found that all banking markets suffered from competition issues, but that these were especially pronounced in the market for SME finance.[3] Cruickshank was not alone: since 2000 there have been over 20 investigations into retail banking, including banking for SMEs, by the Office of Fair Trading (OFT) and the Competition Commission (CC).

Clearly the Government is concerned about the state of the sector. The evidence suggests that the concerns are well-founded and that competition could be decreasing in the wake of the financial crisis. There have been 14 mergers in the banking sector since April 2008, of which the largest was the merger of Lloyds TSB and HBOS to form Lloyds Banking Group. It is not disputed that the banking market is particularly concentrated especially in some products or market areas. RBS, Lloyds, Barclays and HSBC have 78 per cent of the business current account market.[4] These four banks also had a combined market share of 71.1 per cent of SME loans between 2005 and 2008, before the Lloyds – HBOS merger.[5] Consumer markets for savings and current accounts see similar or higher levels of concentration.[6]

Although the banks themselves argue that significant concentration does not automatically result in an uncompetitive market, other aspects of the banking market contribute to a lack of competition. Importantly there are significant barriers to entry and exit, the result of excessive regulatory hurdles for new entrants and incumbent banks being 'too big to fail'. There are also important information asymmetries between customers and providers that do not exist in other concentrated markets such as food retailing. The result of this is that the banks that currently dominate the sector are able to defend the status quo against new entrants, especially in core banking services such as deposit taking, where barriers to entry are highest.

## Failing to serve British businesses

The majority of Britain's banks fail to serve businesses, especially small and medium-sized enterprises (SMEs). The SME market is one of the most concentrated in the banking sector with four banks controlling approximately 80 per cent of the market in 2008, and possibly a greater share since then.[7] The ingrained lack of competition in this sector has increasingly deprived SMEs of high quality banking services. This is of particular concern because SMEs often rely on debt financing to fund investment as they are unable or unwilling to tap equity financing or corporate bond markets.

The lack of competition in the SME banking market has led to the dominance of large banks that dedicate their time and resources to serving larger customers through their investment banking arms. Equally damaging has been the decline in autonomous decision making by branches. An SME visiting one of the branches of Britain's large banks will find that a decision on a loan will not be decided in the branch but by a regional or central office with little or no knowledge of their business. One result has been that the vast majority of the increase in bank lending in the last decade has been for property or to other financial firms rather than to businesses. This is clearly evident in table one.

*Table 1: Lending to businesses (which includes manufacturing and service firms), lending for property (which includes personal mortgages, loans to the construction and real estate sectors) and lending to financial firms (which includes financial intermediation firms and insurance firms) between 2000 and 2010 (£ millions)*

|      | Lending to businesses | Lending for property | Lending to financial firms |
|------|----------------------|----------------------|----------------------------|
| 2000 | 130,500              | 464,258              | 168,377                    |
| 2001 | 127,823              | 514,886              | 171,462                    |
| 2002 | 134,924              | 580,129              | 174,297                    |
| 2003 | 127,821              | 639,782              | 197,213                    |
| 2004 | 124,737              | 690,083              | 244,248                    |
| 2005 | 135,587              | 746,293              | 272,299                    |
| 2006 | 152,411              | 807,014              | 319,371                    |
| 2007 | 161,473              | 871,766              | 455,219                    |
| 2008 | 173,094              | 1,076,548            | 627,014                    |
| 2009 | 163,439              | 1,186,869            | 544,125                    |
| 2010 | 153,294              | 1,285,602            | 467,828                    |

Source: Bank of England statistics, 'Industrial analysis of monetary financial institutions lending to UK residents', 2000-2010

Over the course of the last decade British banks have lent to sectors they viewed as easy and profitable to deal with, shunning what they saw as the difficult task of assessing businesses. Lending to businesses grew by 17.4 per cent, whereas lending for property grew by 176.9 per cent and lending to financial firms grew by 177.8 per cent. This situation is likely to get worse; since the crisis the majority of British banks have dedicated even fewer resources to serving businesses and SMEs in order to repair their balance sheets and increase capital reserves. The data presented indicate that bank lending to businesses fell by £19.8 billion between 2008 and 2010 and there is no indication that the situation improved in 2011. In 2009 Dr Stuart Fraser of Warwick Business School, looking back through the crisis, examined how 2,500 small and medium-sized firms in the UK had been affected. In particular, he examined their experiences between 2001 and 2004 and 2005 and 2008. He also compared the experiences of firms applying for credit in 2008 with those that had applied in the previous three years. He found that:

- Rejection rates amongst SMEs applying for credit had increased;
- this was perhaps a result of rising arrangement fees for loans, which had increased by 21 per cent for 2008 applicants compared to previous years;
- no doubt in response to this and rising interest rates, the use of financial products by SMEs had fallen between 2005 and 2008 compared with 2001 and 2004;
- and without sufficient external financing, between 2005 and 2008, SMEs were using more of their own money to finance investment and day-to-day operations.[8]

Dr Fraser matched firms in his two samples and generated a picture of how credit conditions had changed. By matching firms he was able to eliminate how the riskiness of borrowers affected the terms offered by lenders.

In October 2011 the Office for National Statistics released its 'Access to Finance, 2007 and 2010' survey. The ONS interviewed 77,100 small and medium-sized businesses of different sizes, ages and across different industries on whether they had sought finance in 2007 and 2010 and whether they had been successful. Businesses reported that:

- 42 per cent had sought finance in 2010, up from 35 per cent in 2007;
- of these, 27 per cent sought loan finance, up from 22 per cent in 2007;
- in both 2007 and 2010 approximately 75 per cent of loan finance was sourced from banks;
- in 2007, 74 per cent of businesses sought finance and 65 per cent were successful. The result was that 88 per cent of business that applied for finance received it;
- in 2010, 77 per cent of businesses sought finance and only 49 per cent were successful. The result was that 63 per cent of business that applied for finance received it;
- 89 per cent of fast growing businesses[9] were successful in obtaining loan finance in 2007 yet only 50 per cent were successful in 2010.

The ONS' survey reinforces Dr Fraser's findings. All businesses were finding it more difficult to obtain finance in 2010 than 2007. It is particularly worrying that fast growing businesses saw the most dramatic fall in loan finance success rates as these companies generate jobs at a faster rate than other businesses. The ONS' findings also provide a useful picture of how credit conditions have developed; they indicate that banks are still failing to serve the real economy.

The Bank of England's monthly 'Trends in Lending' publication uses data from monetary and financial institutions to assess the state of the British credit market. The latest edition covers lending up until August 2011, and reports that:

- Annual lending growth was negative in August 2011 at -3.3 per cent[10] and this figure was -5 per cent for SMEs;[11]
- the indicative median interest rate on new SME lending has remained relatively constant since mid-2009, at around 3.5 per cent;[12]

- however, the indicative median interest rate for smaller SMEs, those with an annual bank account debit turnover of under £1 million, increased from below 4 per cent to nearly 5 per cent between mid-2008 and September 2011.[13]

There is some debate as to what extent this contraction in credit reflects reduced demand by businesses or reduced supply and increased margins by lenders. Yet the evidence provided by the Bank of England suggests that loan costs remain an issue, especially for small businesses. This conclusion is buttressed by the fact that in every edition of the Bank of England's 'Credit Conditions Survey' since the third quarter of 2010, lenders have indicated that they expect the price of credit to increase for small businesses.[14]

The credit crunch continues in Britain today despite the fact that lending to businesses accounts for a miniscule part of the assets of Britain's goliath banks. The economist John Kay estimates that the assets and liabilities of British banks exceed £6 trillion while lending to businesses accounts for £200 billion, or 3 per cent of the total.[15] Britain's banks, despite or even perhaps because of their size, are no longer suited to supporting British businesses. This concern is widely shared. For example, in May 2011 the Business Secretary Vince Cable said 'there is a serious problem with lending to good, small companies'.[16] Furthermore, there is a widely held view that the current banks cannot be simply cajoled into lending more to SMEs. Prime Minister David Cameron said in November 2010:

> You can go for lending agreements with the banks. The trouble is, what I find with lending agreements is that they will promise to do a certain amount of lending to one sector, but they'll shrink it somewhere else.[17]

There are growing calls for new banks or new mechanisms for delivering credit to SMEs. In September 2011 Adam Posen of the Bank of England's Monetary Policy Committee called for two Government institutions to be set up:

> One would be a public bank or authority for lending to small business [which] would in the first instance be choosing among loan applications already rejected by pre-existing banks.[18]

The other institution would collect and securitise loans to SMEs to increase liquidity in the market. Clearly there are widespread calls for significant reform of Britain's banking sector due in part to concerns with improving services for SMEs. The problem is that despite recognising the failings of the incumbent banks, politicians have taken no decisive action.

*Failing consumers*

Britain's large banks are not just unpopular with British businesses, they are very often disliked by individual customers. Which?, the consumer campaigning charity, conducted a poll of approximately 13,000 people earlier this year asking which British banks offered the best customer service. The poll quizzed respondents on how satisfied they were with their current account, mortgage, savings and credit card providers. It also asked how likely they were to recommend providers to a friend or family member. None of Britain's large banks were at the top of the poll and Halifax and Bank of Scotland, both owned by Lloyds, were placed near the bottom.[19] Similar results were recorded the previous year.[20]

One interesting aspect of the results is that some of the banks that polled high are actually owned by the large banks that scored so badly. The number-one bank in 2011, First Direct, is owned by HSBC and the One Account received a satisfaction score of 81 per cent in 2010 while its owner, RBS, scored 53 per cent. Both First Direct and the One Account, although owned by HSBC and RBS respectively, are independent subsidiaries and both are intensely customer-oriented with little concern other than providing relatively simple products to consumers. By contrast RBS, HSBC and other universal banks offer investment banking, wealth management, retail banking services, and others. As a result they spread resources across different departments, often in a way that neglects the retail segment of the business. As a consequence less attention is paid to improving customer service because it is just one of many competing concerns. Many of Britain's banks, but especially those that have merged with other firms or added different business units over time, have incredibly convoluted business structures that inhibit their capacity to offer good customer service.

This is evident when one considers how difficult it can be for customers of the dominant high-street banks. Anyone who has used telephone banking will know how very rarely one operator can deal with more than one request. This is the result of outdated IT systems that have been built up over the years and are in need of an overhaul. Different departments have different IT systems. Not all operators can access these systems and so must transfer callers to other operators when a different request needs to be dealt with. A refusal to engage in expensive IT restructuring has also resulted in the vast majority of Britain's large banks being incredibly slow at embracing new technologies. The Faster Payments service, a new interbank payments system, was launched in May 2008 and should provide banks with the ability to transfer payments between them in seconds, clearing them in hours rather than days. However, Britain's big banks have been slow to adopt the system across all transactions, while the lack of competition allows them to continue to charge business customers the same amount that they always have for what is now a poor quality service. Diane Coyle, previously a member of the Competition Commission, drew attention to this issue in her response to the ICB:

> At the same time, the absence of competition has meant that while the banks have had every opportunity to take advantage of customers through excessive charges and fees and inappropriate products, there has been none of the dynamic innovation that would have occurred in a competitive market. Thus while people from Singapore to Kenya can use a new range of payments technologies, British banks have been slow bringing these innovations to their customers – and when they do so they manage to put the (hidden) fees up, rather than bringing them down.[21]

It is indicative of the problem described above that in a survey of 14 high street banks in the UK, conducted in June 2011, only four had a mobile phone application offering banking services.[22]

## *The opportunities for new banks*

Why do large banks continue to dominate the market despite the compelling evidence that they do not provide particularly good customer service? On the whole their continued dominance is the result of significant barriers to entry and these barriers are examined in detail in chapter six. However, the present circumstances and developments in banking do suggest that now could be a propitious time for new banks to challenge the incumbents.

The outdated IT systems of the large banks are a burden that new entrants would not have to bear. New banks could use up-to-date systems and the newest technology. Such technology has already helped credit unions and local banks in America, allowing them to challenge the commercial banks. Products such as the 'Kasasa' account service developed by the American firm BankVue allows customers to access their accounts and carry out transactions at any bank that uses the Kasasa system. This has increased the operating scale of local banks and credit unions.

Many British banks also suffer from an inefficient use of their branch network. It is often said that in a world where many banking activities can be carried out online or over the telephone, branches are a financial burden rather than a benefit. Such an argument ignores the fact that a significant number of people still choose to interact with their bank primarily through the branch and that branch staff can provide services and expertise that cannot be delivered remotely. Nevertheless, it is the case that the internet has changed many other service industries, the decline of travel agents providing a useful example, and that surviving in a digital age will increasingly require a physical business to offer a valuable face-to-face service that cannot be delivered online. For a bank this is likely to be the expertise that goes with assessing small business loans or providing expertise on complex products, while continuing to serve customers that may not want, or be able, to access remote banking services. The majority of Britain's large banks do not appear to have grasped this fact other than by simply closing branches.[23] This provides new entrants with two opportunities. Firstly, new banks can use remote delivery channels such as the internet, mobile phone applications and telephone banking to serve customers at a lower cost. The success of many online savings accounts and branchless banks such as First Direct is testament to this. Second, new banks can offer better branch banking than the dominant banks, although perhaps through fewer branches. The early success of Metro Bank illustrates how branch banking can be redefined and the continued success of the Swedish Bank Handelsbanken, discussed in greater detail in chapter five, demonstrates how a commercial bank can make the branch the most effective business unit.

The combination of customer dissatisfaction and public anger provides a fantastic opportunity to reform the British banking market.

Politicians have a popular mandate for reform and consumers are likely to vote with their feet to support new, better, banks. This opportunity could be wasted if the Government does not remove the barriers to entry that are stifling competition and take active steps to encourage the development of local banks that can provide a real alternative to the dominant British banks. The following chapters will examine alternative local banks, each of which could provide the whole, or part, of a blueprint for a network of British local banks. For such a network to develop, the Government needs to remove the barriers to entry that protect the current banking oligopoly and take steps that will allow local banks to challenge it.

# 2. Swiss Cantonal banks

*Serving the Swiss economy*

When one thinks of Swiss Banking, UBS and Credit Suisse may come to mind along with hedge funds, private equity and 'secret' Swiss bank accounts. This is just one side of Switzerland's financial sector, a side that concentrates on serving international customers and operates in international markets. Switzerland's domestic economy and many domestic customers, individuals and businesses, are served by institutions such as the cooperative banks (Raiffeisen), regional banks and more importantly the Cantonal banks.

Switzerland is divided into 26 cantons, highly independent federal states that have their own legislatures, constitutions, courts and governments. Twenty-four cantons also have their own Cantonal bank. The 24 Cantonal banks, members of the Association of Swiss Cantonal Banks (ASCB), conduct approximately 90 per cent of their operations in Switzerland.[24]

The assets and liabilities of the Swiss Cantonal banks reveal how important they are to the Swiss economy.

*Table 2: Selected assets and liabilities of the Cantonal Banks and Large Commercial Banks in Switzerland (CHF billions) (£1/1.4CHF 2012)*

|  | Large Commercial Banks | | Cantonal Banks | | All Swiss banks |
| --- | --- | --- | --- | --- | --- |
|  | CHF billions | % | CHF billions | % | CHF billions |
| Balance sheet total | 1,482.1 | 100 | 421.5 | 100 | **2,714.5** |
| Liabilities towards customers | 631.8 | 42.6 | 258.6 | 61.3 | **1,389.2** |
| Of which are savings and deposits | 123.7 | 8.3 | 158.3 | 37.6 | **456.6** |
| Asset claims against customers and mortgage claims | 552.6 | 37.3 | 307.5 | 73.0 | **1,284.3** |

Source: Swiss National Bank, Banks in Switzerland 2010

The two large commercial banks are far larger than the Cantonal banks. Despite this, the Cantonal banks take in more savings and deposits than the large commercial banks, and total 'liabilities towards customers' account for a far larger part of their balance sheets. In terms of assets the situation is almost identical. Over three quarters of the total balance sheets of the Cantonal banks are composed of asset claims against customers, whereas this figure is only 46.9 per cent for UBS and Credit Suisse. Their asset and liability structure is indicative of the business model of the Cantonal banks: they take local deposits and lend locally to businesses and individuals.

In the domestic market, the Cantonal banks 'punch above their weight'. Relative to their size, the Cantonal banks dedicate more resources to serving domestic customers and the Swiss economy than the two large commercial banks. Despite accounting for only 15.5 per cent of Swiss bank assets and liabilities, the Cantonal banks account for 18.6 per cent of liabilities towards customers, 34.7 per cent of savings and deposits and 20.6 per cent of asset claims against customers.[25]

In 2010 the Cantonal banks became the most significant providers of credit to the Swiss economy, accounting for 32.7 per cent of the total domestic loan volume of Swiss banks, including mortgage lending.[26] Excluding mortgage lending the Cantonal banks accounted for 27.7 per cent of the Swiss lending market.[27] A previous study examining lending in 2002 found a similar figure,[28] and this figure echoes analysis by the ASCB that the market share of the Cantonal banks is about one third, depending on the business area.[29]

Although the Cantonal banks have around a quarter to a third of the market for domestic loans, the majority of SMEs tend to have a relationship with a Cantonal bank. This is the case even though Cantonal banks can only serve SMEs that operate in their canton. Using a representative sample of Swiss SMEs, Doris Neuberger and Christoph Schacht estimate that 80 per cent of medium-sized firms,[30] 58 per cent of small firms[31] and 45 per cent of micro firms[32] have a lending relationship with a Cantonal bank.[33] It is worth bearing in mind that a greater number of medium-sized firms have a lending relationship with a Cantonal bank because a successful small firm will often maintain its relationship with its Cantonal bank as it grows in size. Neuberger and Schacht also found similar results for the large commercial banks, nevertheless it is clear that relative to the size of their balance sheets the Cantonal banks dedicate greater resources to serving SMEs. To understand why this is the case one needs to look at the governance structure and business model of the Cantonal banks.

## *The constitution of the Swiss Cantonal banks*

There are 24 Cantonal banks. Originally, a Cantonal bank served each of Switzerland's 26 cantons, however the Canton Appenzell Ausserrhoden sold its bank to UBS in 1996 and the Canton Solothurn privatised its bank in 1995. In both cases the banks ran into financial difficulties and, as a response, were sold off. Both sales were directly approved by the electorates through plebiscites that changed the cantonal constitutions to allow the sales to go ahead.

Despite belonging to the ASCB the Cantonal banks vary in size and activity. The Banque Cantonal de Jura is the smallest Cantonal bank with a balance sheet of only CHF 2.17 billion.[34] The bank serves businesses and individuals in the Canton of Jura providing mortgages, savings accounts, loans, pensions and wealth management services.[35] In contrast the Zürcher Kantonalbank, the largest Cantonal bank, has a balance sheet of CHF 130.06 billion and accounts for nearly a third of the total assets of the Cantonal banks.[36] The Zürcher Kantonalbank competes with Switzerland's large commercial banks and has representatives and advisory offices in a number of other countries.

In addition to size and services offered, the Cantonal banks also vary in terms of legal form, although the Swiss Government sets ownership restrictions for the banks. The Swiss Federal Constitution gives the Swiss Government the power to 'legislate on the banking and stock exchange system; in doing so, it shall take account of the special function and role of the Cantonal banks'.[37] In carrying out this responsibility the Federal Government enacted the Swiss Federal Law on Banks and Savings Banks in 1934. Article 3a of this act defines the constitutional arrangements of the Cantonal banks:

> A bank which is constituted in the form of an establishment or limited-liability company on the basis of a Cantonal legal ordinance shall be deemed to be a Cantonal bank. The Canton must hold a participation of more than one third of capital and possess more than one third of the voting rights. The Canton may guarantee, either in full or in part, for the liabilities of the bank.[38]

The article allows for banks to be partially, wholly or majority-owned by their canton, but in practice Cantonal banks are either wholly or majority owned by their canton. Eleven of the banks are wholly-owned by their canton, eleven are companies with publicly traded shares and two are companies whose stock is privately traded.[39]

Each canton is responsible for defining its Cantonal bank's ownership structure and how it will operate. Geneva's Cantonal legal ordinance the 'Law on Banque Cantonale de Genève' of 24 June 1993 defines the Cantonal bank as a public limited company principally operating within, and serving, the Canton of Geneva and the surrounding region. The operations of the bank are guaranteed by the Cantonal Government, although unlike some other Cantonal banks this guarantee is limited in terms of size and by category of depositor.[40] The bank is run by a professional Executive Board whose activities are overseen by the Board of Directors. The Board of Directors 'must, as far as possible, reflect the different tendencies of the Canton's economic and social life'[41] and include representatives from the Cantonal Government, municipal governments and other shareholders. The Board of Directors ensures that the bank is serving the Cantonal economy but cannot get involved in the commercial operations of the bank. The Cantonal Government holds a majority of the shares although a portion is allowed to be publicly and privately traded.[42]

The governing structure of Geneva Cantonal bank is representative of the other Cantonal banks, the most important features being the Board of Directors and the fact that bank is majority-owned by the canton. These are not the only mechanisms which encourage localism on the part of the Cantonal banks. Cantonal banks with publicly traded shares often take steps to increase local shareholding, the Cantonal bank of Zug states on its website that:

> We know our shareholders. Our traded common shares are owned 50% by the canton and 50% in the hands of over 7,000 stockholders, predominantly from the Canton Zug. We want to maintain this structure, with a broad, regionally anchored shareholder base.[43]

One way of doing this is to give share preference to customers who have a bank account, a tactic employed by the Cantonal bank of

St. Gall.[44] As a result, the majority of individual and institutional shareholders of the Cantonal banks reside in the canton. In a 2007 study of six Cantonal banks, 85.3 per cent of individual shareholders and 77.5 per cent of institutional shareholders resided in the home canton of the bank.[45]

The Swiss Cantonal banks are not subject to significant government involvement: although the Board of Directors does include government representation, the chairman cannot be drawn from government. More importantly, the Board of Directors can only enforce the legal ordinances and cantonal constitution which commits the banks to serve the cantonal economy while turning a profit. Switzerland's Cantonal banks are regulated, like all other banks and financial intermediaries, by the Swiss Financial Market Supervisory Authority (FINMA). They are bound by the same capital and liquidity rules and all other regulations. Like Switzerland's commercial banks, the Cantonal banks are still driven by commercial concerns but must balance these against the requirement, laid down in law, which forces them to serve their local economies. The next section makes it clear that this balance is successfully achieved.

## *Success and stability*

The financial crisis took its toll on some Swiss banks, in particular UBS which lost over CHF 20 billion in 2008.[46] The crisis however provided the Cantonal banks with an opportunity to expand. With the large commercial banks suffering heavy losses customers looked to safer competitors, and it was no surprise that many flocked to the Cantonal banks that were in a far better shape to weather the crisis. The resilience displayed by the Cantonal banks over the last few years is not the result of the cantonal government support that many enjoy. Fourteen Cantonal banks have to pay for their cantonal guarantee, whereas the implicit support afforded to the large commercial banks helped lower their funding costs in the run up to the crisis. The Cantonal banks were in a far better shape before the financial crisis because their capital reserves significantly exceeded the regulatory minimum.

*Table 3: Excess capital of the Cantonal Banks and Large Commercial Banks as a percentage of the required capital (%)*

|      | Large Commercial Banks | Cantonal Banks |
| ---- | ---------------------- | -------------- |
| 2002 | 36.3                   | 35.8           |
| 2003 | 25.7                   | 57.9           |
| 2004 | 25.0                   | 72.9           |
| 2005 | 25.1                   | 85.7           |
| 2006 | 42.7                   | 89.1           |
| 2007 | 20.4                   | 95.7           |
| 2008 | 67.4                   | 95.5           |
| 2009 | 132.3                  | 100.3          |
| 2010 | 114.6                  | 94.0           |

Source: Swiss National Bank, Banks in Switzerland 2010

The Cantonal banks approached the crisis with far higher levels of capital than the two large commercial banks. In 2007 before the crisis hit, the large commercial banks had capital reserves above the regulatory minimum of 20.4 per cent. In contrast, the Cantonal banks had 'excess capital' of 95.7 per cent. As the crisis unfolded the large commercial banks increased their capital reserves with the help of the Swiss Government which injected vast sums of money into the banks, especially UBS.

Although their links with the cantonal governments helped create a positive public perception of the safety of the Cantonal banks, their financial position before the crisis allowed them to expand during it. Without their capital cushion the Cantonal banks would have struggled to capture more of the Swiss mortgage and savings markets.

*Table 4: Savings and deposits and mortgages of the Cantonal Banks and Large Commercial Banks (CHF billions)*

|      | Cantonal Banks        |           | Large Commercial Banks |           |
| ---- | --------------------- | --------- | ---------------------- | --------- |
|      | Savings and deposits  | Mortgages | Savings and deposits   | Mortgages |
| 2006 | 111.5                 | 216.9     | 116.1                  | 222.1     |
| 2007 | 104.8                 | 221.8     | 105.2                  | 225.4     |
| 2008 | 125.0                 | 229.9     | 96.6                   | 228.1     |
| 2009 | 148.2                 | 245.8     | 115.4                  | 231.2     |
| 2010 | 158.3                 | 260.1     | 123.7                  | 234.0     |

Source: Swiss National Bank, Banks in Switzerland 2010

In 2006 the Cantonal banks had a smaller share of the savings and mortgage markets than the two large commercial banks yet by 2008 they had the largest share of both markets. The Cantonal banks have gone on to increase their share of the market as customers have increasingly recognised their superior service and security and as a result of the large commercial banks scaling back services as they rebuild their balance sheets.

Their success during the crisis was undoubtedly a boon to the ASCB but more importantly it was immensely beneficial to the Swiss economy. The British economy has floundered since the financial crisis as a result of banks being unwilling to lend at acceptable prices. As a consequence SMEs have been particularly affected by falling credit levels. In a similar way to Britain's large commercial banks, UBS and Credit Suisse also scaled back their operations and reduced lending to businesses as a result of the crisis; however Switzerland found that the Cantonal banks were able to partially fill the gap.

*Table 5: Credit provided by Swiss banks (excluding mortgage credit) (CHF billions)*

|  | Large Commercial Banks | Cantonal Banks |
|---|---|---|
| 2006 | 134.0 | 38.4 |
| 2007 | 174.9 | 41.1 |
| 2008 | 157.0 | 45.1 |
| 2009 | 127.7 | 46.0 |
| 2010 m2 | 135.3 | 47.0 |
| 2010 m5 | 136.1 | 47.5 |
| 2010 m7 | 114.0 | 46.5 |
| 2010 m9 | 111.7 | 47.1 |
| 2010 m11 | 114.6 | 47.6 |
| 2011 m2 | 112.7 | 48.1 |
| 2011 m5 | 110.6 | 48.0 |
| 2011 m7 | 107.5 | 47.3 |

Source: Swiss National Bank, Monthly Bulletin of Banking Statistics September 2011

The large commercial banks reduced lending by 38.5 per cent from a peak in 2007 to July 2011. Over the same period, the Cantonal banks increased lending by 15.2 per cent. The Cantonal banks continued to lend despite the fact that fewer of their loans were secured. In July 2011, 49.7 per cent of the loans of the large commercial banks were unsecured compared to 73.0 per cent for the Cantonal banks.[47] This is a testament to their business model and effective risk management systems that rely on sound knowledge of local borrowers.

*Table 6: Profit and loss account of the Cantonal Banks and the Large Commercial Banks (CHF millions)*

|  | Cantonal Banks | | Large Commercial Banks | |
| --- | --- | --- | --- | --- |
|  | Profits for the year | Losses for the year | Profits for the year | Losses for the year |
| 2003 | 1,207.0 | | 7,053.3 | |
| 2004 | 1,576.2 | | 9,360.9 | |
| 2005 | 2,017.9 | | 17,006.7 | |
| 2006 | 2,416.1 | | 10,911.4 | |
| 2007 | 2,626.7 | | 2,847.4 | −4,251.2[48] |
| 2008 | 2,157.3 | −56.8 | | −38,185.2 |
| 2009 | 2,349.7 | | 377.5 | −5,041.3 |
| 2010 | 2,605.6 | | 6,123.2 | −2,674.1 |
| **Total Profit (profits-losses)** | **16,900.2** | | **3,528.5** | |

Source: Swiss National Bank, Banks in Switzerland 2010

Between 2003 and 2010 the Cantonal banks made a profit of CHF 16.9 billion and the large commercial banks, UBS and Credit Suisse, made a profit of CHF 3.5 billion. This is remarkable especially when one takes into account the fact that the Cantonal banks are so much smaller. The fluctuations in the profits of the large commercial banks meant that their performance varied dramatically between 2003 and 2010; in contrast the profits of the Cantonal banks remained far more consistent. It could be argued that these figures are unique given the huge losses suffered by the large commercial banks, particularly UBS, during the financial crisis. Nevertheless, they do accurately portray the stability, constancy and profitability of the Cantonal banks.

The Swiss Cantonal banks are not an isolated or unusual example of banks that manage to balance stability and service to the local economy with profit. Furthermore, many of their important features – their locally-orientated business model, balancing of profit and stability, and oversight by the Board of Directors – are found in the German Sparkassen.

# 3. The German Sparkassen

*Serving the German economy*

Germany is a good example of a banking system marked by variety and is often described as 'three-pillared'. The three pillars are the private commercial banks, such as Deutsche Bank or Commerzbank, the cooperative banks (Volks-und Raiffeisenbanken) and the public banks. The last group is subdivided into Landesbanks (German Federal State banks) and Sparkassen (savings banks).

Similar to Switzerland, the large commercial banks tend to concentrate on larger, international businesses and wealthier individuals, with the Sparkassen and cooperative banks serving SMEs and the vast majority of the population. A similar picture to Switzerland emerges when the assets and liabilities of the Sparkassen and large commercial banks are examined.

*Table 7: Selected assets and liabilities of the Large Commercial Banks and the Sparkassen (£1/€1.2, 2012)*

|  | Large Commercial Banks |  | Sparkassen |  |
| --- | --- | --- | --- | --- |
|  | € billion | % | € billion | % |
| **Liabilities** | 2,138.1 | 100 | 1,078.2 | 100 |
| Deposits of banks | 458.1 | 21.4 | 178.3 | 16.5 |
| Deposits of non-banks | 539.3 | 25.2 | 755.9 | 70.1 |
| Other liabilities | 902.4 | 42.2 | 57.5 | 5.3 |
| **Assets** | 2,138.1 | 100 | 1,078.2 | 100 |
| Lending to banks | 581.4 | 27.2 | 246.8 | 22.9 |
| Lending to non-banks | 542.8 | 25.4 | 775.7 | 71.9 |
| Other assets | 932.6 | 43.6 | 17.7 | 1.6 |

Source: Deutsche Bundesbank, Monthly Report as of October 14, 2011

The Sparkassen dedicate their resources to serving households and local businesses whereas the large commercial banks dedicate far more resources to serving other banks. Very few of the assets and liabilities of the Sparkassen are contained within the 'other' categories, whereas the large commercial banks see almost half of their balance sheet made up of 'other' items. This is representative of the varying business models: the Sparkassen engage in mortgage and business lending, savings, investment and current accounts, as well as some asset management and more sophisticated services to businesses; the large commercial banks engage in investment banking and trading services for their clients, activities captured in the 'other' liabilities and assets categories.

*Table 8: Lending to different industries by the Sparkassen and Large Commercial Banks (as a percentage of total lending)*

| Industry | Sparkassen | Large Commercial Banks |
|---|---|---|
| **Chemicals, Minerals, Oils** | **0.5** | **1.5** |
| Rubber and Synthetic | 0.6 | 0.5 |
| Glass and Ceramic Production | 0.5 | 0.6 |
| Metal Production | 2.5 | 2.6 |
| **Mechanical, Engineering** | **1.8** | **4.8** |
| **Data Processing, Electrical Devices** | **0.9** | **2.1** |
| Wood, Paper, Furniture | 2.2 | 1.8 |
| Textiles, Clothes, Leather | 0.3 | 0.5 |
| Food and Tobacco | 1.6 | 1.5 |
| Energy, Water Supply/Disposal | 5.2 | 5.6 |
| Construction Industry | 7.7 | 1.6 |
| Car trade and maintenance | 11.5 | 8.4 |
| Agriculture, Forestry | 3.1 | 0.6 |
| **Transport, Storage** | **3.1** | **5.5** |
| **Insurance, Finance** | **5.7** | **25.2** |
| Building/Housing Society | 13.9 | 6.6 |
| Holding/Investment | 2.6 | 4.6 |
| Other Land property | 13.3 | 10.0 |
| Hotels and Restaurants | 3.0 | 9.1 |
| Health Veterinary | 6.0 | 3.8 |
| Removable Goods | 0.6 | 1.1 |
| Other Services | 4.2 | 2.8 |
| **Total** | **100** | **100** |

Source: Source: Deutsche Bundesbank, Bankenstatistik Stand vom 15.8.2011

This is not to suggest that the large commercial banks are wholly-outward facing and completely fail to serve the German economy. They do, however, serve different types of individuals and businesses. One of the strengths of the German banking market is that the diverse needs of customers are met by different banks. Britain does not benefit from such variety.

Table eight shows lending to domestic enterprises, grouped into different industries, by the Sparkassen and large commercial banks. Figures are given as a percentage of total lending by each group of banks to indicate the degree to which specific industries are being served. It is worth bearing in mind that the total loan volume of the Sparkassen in the second quarter of 2011 was €322.3 billion compared to €177.3 billion for the large commercial banks. The sectors in bold are those where the commercial banks lent more than the Sparkassen in absolute as well as percentage terms. The large commercial banks tend to lend to sectors dominated by larger, more capital intensive firms, including engineering and chemical businesses and firms producing electrical devices. It is particularly important that over a quarter of the total lending volume of the commercial banks is directed towards the finance and insurance industries.

In contrast the loans of the Sparkassen are more evenly spread. Importantly, the Sparkassen lend far more to the agricultural and fisheries industries, to hotels and restaurants, the construction industry and to tradespeople across different industries. The Sparkassen serve businesses and sectors that are not seen as sufficiently profitable by the large commercial banks. SMEs are particularly well served and around 75 per cent of German SMEs have a relationship with a sparkasse.[49] As a result more small and new German businesses have access to credit than in the UK. In Germany, start-ups obtain approximately 27 per cent of their finance from their bank, whereas this figure is only 12 per cent for British start-ups.[50] It is not hard to understand why British businesses, used to being rejected for loans by banks that have pulled all resources out of 'unprofitable' or 'risky' sectors, look yearningly at the German Sparkassen.

## The constitution of the Sparkassen

The Sparkassen are part of the Sparkassen-Finanzgruppe. Germany is a federal state with sixteen states or 'Länder'. The Sparkassen-Finanzgruppe is itself a federation in which the Landesbanken[51] (banks of the Federal States of Germany) provide the Sparkassen with wholesale banking services and liquidity management. They also act as the banks of the various Land governments. The group also includes a number of other financial firms offering investments, leasing, insurance and other services. The Landesbanken are different to the Sparkassen and their balance sheets resemble those of the large commercial banks. During the financial crisis a number of Landesbanken ran into difficulties through purchasing US mortgage securities and had to be bailed out by the German Government. As well as acting as the central banks of the Sparkassen, the Landesbanken also provide services to customers that cannot be provided by the Sparkassen such as large loans or investment banking services. Recently some of the Landesbanken have been more of a burden than a benefit to the savings bank network and they would better serve the group if they moved their business model back towards that of the Sparkassen.

The Sparkassen are institutions with a unique legal form, outlined in German Federal Laws but more predominantly in the laws of the individual Länder. Section 40 of the Banking Act of the Federal Republic of Germany, drawn up in 1961, sets down which banks can be set up as savings banks:

(1) public savings banks holding a licence in accordance with section 32;[52]

(2) other enterprises which were legitimately using such a term under former regulations;

(3) enterprises which by virtue of their articles of association, display special features (in particular, business objectives geared to the common weal and a restriction of their principal activities to the economic locality in which the enterprise is domiciled).[53]

The Banking Act makes it very clear that a savings bank must have 'business objectives geared to the common weal'. This idea is fleshed out in more detail in the specific savings bank laws of the individual Länder, but it ensures that the Sparkassen follow what has been described as a 'dual bottom line' approach to business.[54] The two bottom lines that must be pursued are profit and 'objectives geared to the common weal'. Neither has precedence, profit is a necessary part of a viable and sustainable business but, for a Sparkassen, profit must be generated by serving the bank's local community and economy.

The Banking Act also states that the activities of each Sparkasse must be restricted to the 'economic locality in which the enterprise is domiciled'. This principle of geographic exclusivity is sometimes criticised as being uncompetitive, but the Sparkassen have remained competitive despite the fact that German consumers have several alternative banks available – far more than the British consumer. By restricting competition between Sparkassen, the principle of geographic exclusivity or 'Regionalitätsprinzip' aligns the interests of the savings bank and the local community and ensures that the bank concentrates on providing the best possible service to their local economy.

The aims and operating ethos of the Sparkassen are further elaborated in the constitutions of the individual Länder. Section 2, clause 2 of the Thuringian Savings Bank Act (ThürSpKG) applies to all Sparkassen in the Free State of Thuringia:

**Business aims, public remit**

(1) Savings banks are businesses serving the common good with the task to ensure the provision of financial services within their sector, in particular to provide opportunity for secure financial investment. Savings banks strengthen competition within the financial sector. They provide services for the public, the economy, in particular the middle classes* and the public services, in due consideration of the requirements of the markets. They support positive attitudes towards saving, accumulation of wealth and the monetary education of the young.

(2) Savings banks conduct business under the guidance of the Savings Banks Act and represent the interest of their clients. Business regarding central savings banks, mortgage banks, regarding property, investment and insurance should be pursued in collaboration with the respective branches of the Organisation of Savings Banks in Thuringia.

(3) Savings banks conduct their business following the principles and standard practices of business, under due consideration of their public remit. Profit is not the main purpose of their business.[55]

---

*Middle class should be read as 'Mittelstand' here. When the laws were drafted middle class was meant to describe the tradespeople, small, medium and family-owned businesses that now make up the 'Mittelstand' sector of the German economy.

The Act makes clear that the Sparkassen must 'strengthen competition' and provide services for the 'Mittelstand', the community of small and medium-sized, as well as family-owned enterprises. The Act also makes it very clear that 'profit is not the main purpose of their business'. The Sparkassen are guided by the legal requirement to serve SMEs, local customers and groups at risk of financial exclusion. If they fail to do so, a bank's executives can be brought to task by the Administrative Council or Supervisory Board of the bank. Like all other German banks the Sparkassen are regulated by the Federal Financial Services Authority (BaFin) and the German Central Bank (Deutsche Bundesbank), and must adhere to the same regulatory standards as all other financial institutions.

Unlike the Swiss Cantonal banks the Sparkassen are all municipal bodies with no shareholders. Like the Cantonal banks the Sparkassen are all overseen by an Administrative Council or Supervisory Board that ensures the bank is sticking to its legal remit. Two thirds of the membership of the Supervisory Board is appointed by the municipal council and the remaining third is appointed by the bank's employees. It is the job of the Supervisory Board to make sure that the executives of the bank conduct business in accordance with Federal and Länd statutes. In this context, the Supervisory Board is akin to the Board of Directors in a Cantonal bank. Similar oversight was provided by trustees in one of Britain's main banks until the 1980s, though this will be examined in greater detail in chapter four.

*Credit Guarantees*

The Sparkassen, along with Germany's other banks, benefit from an effective system of credit guarantees for loans. The system is run by guarantee banks that were set up by trade associations after WWII. In some respects, the guarantee banks operate like the British Government's Enterprise Finance Guarantee and its predecessor, the Small Firms Loan Guarantee. However, the German system is far more effective.

The guarantee banks are not-for-profit institutions owned by trade associations, banks, insurance companies and other financial backers. The 18 banks organise themselves through the Association of German

Guarantee Banks (VDB). The banks confine their activities to the specific German Land in which they operate. The principle of geographic exclusivity encourages each bank to cultivate local knowledge and industry expertise that improves the service they offer to local businesses.[56]

The guarantee banks issue sureties that cover loans or guarantees that cover equity investments. As with the Enterprise Finance Guarantee these cover a proportion of the loan or investment. However, unlike the British scheme, the guarantees are not wholly funded by the Government. When a guarantee bank issues a surety they take on 20-35 per cent of the risk and the rest is borne by the Federal and Land governments. The distribution of risk is similar for a guarantee.[57] The guarantee banks serve established businesses as well as start-ups and a firm can seek a guarantee before or after they approach a lender. The borrower has to pay a one-off processing fee equal to 1.0-1.5 per cent of the guaranteed credit amount and an annual guarantee commission equal to 1.0-1.5 per cent of the amount outstanding.

To help more businesses access credit, the German Government increased its support for the VDB during the financial crisis by increasing its share of outstanding guarantees by 10 per cent, increasing the maximum guarantee per company from €1 million to €2 million and increasing the maximum guarantee from 80 per cent to 90 per cent of a loan. The guarantee banks also increased the upper limit of their share of the guarantee to 50 per cent.

In contrast to the Enterprise Finance Guarantee, which saw lending reach an all-time low in December 2011,[58] research indicates that the VDB is making an important contribution to the German economy. Two independent reports by the Institut für Mittelstandsökonomie an der Universität Trier (Institute for SMEs at the University of Trier) in 2006 and 2009 supported this conclusion and found that in 2006 only 5 per cent of companies who had obtained a guarantee would have received a loan without one.[59] In an average year between 2000 and 2009, the VDB covered loans and investments worth €1.1 billion.[60] The return on these loans and investments was calculated at three times their original amount.[61] Importantly the VDB helps SMEs and start-ups and works in tandem with the Sparkassen. Between 1994 and 2004 30 per cent of the VDB's guarantees went to start-ups[62] and 60 per cent of the VDB's guarantees in 2009 covered loans provided by the Sparkassen and German cooperative banks.[63]

The success of Germany's guarantee banks stands in stark contrast to the failure of the UK's Enterprise Finance Guarantee. It also indicates how an effective credit guarantee system, operating at a local level, can support local banks.

## Resilient and profitable

The financial crisis was described as a 'credit crunch' because many banks stopped or reduced lending to the wider economy. The impressive thing about the Sparkassen is that they continued to lend throughout the crisis.

*Table 9: Lending volumes during the financial crisis by the Sparkassen and Large Commercial Banks (€ billions)*

|         | Sparkassen | Large Commercial Banks |
|---------|------------|------------------------|
| 2006-01 | 275.5      | 196.6                  |
| 2006-07 | 276.8      | 201.9                  |
| 2007-01 | 276.1      | 191.2                  |
| 2007-07 | 280.6      | 189.3                  |
| 2008-01 | 286.0      | 199.1                  |
| 2008-07 | 294.4      | 198.8                  |
| 2009-01 | 299.2      | 183.9                  |
| 2009-07 | 305.4      | 189.6                  |
| 2010-01 | 309.1      | 173.3                  |
| 2010-07 | 315.1      | 170.7                  |
| 2011-01 | 319.3      | 168.9                  |
| 2011-04 | 322.3      | 177.2                  |

Source: Deutsche Bundesbank, Lending to domestic enterprises and self-employed persons, 2011

Table nine shows the lending volumes of the Sparkassen and large commercial banks since the beginning of 2006. The Sparkassen increased their volume of loans by 17.0 per cent while the large commercial banks reduced loan volume by 9.8 per cent.[64] As the

German economy looked to bounce back from the financial crisis, the Sparkassen consistently provided credit to businesses looking to increase production. The German economy shrank by 4.7 per cent in 2009 and yet grew by 3.6 per cent in 2010.[65] The dramatic turnaround in 2010 was the result of businesses utilising spare capacity that had lain dormant when demand dropped in 2009. Businesses were able to do so because they had the necessary capital to expand production, a disproportionate amount of which came from the Sparkassen that continued to lend during this difficult period. Having gone through the financial crisis relatively unscathed, the Sparkassen were not stuck repairing their balance sheets and could support the real economy. Britain's large banks, battered by the crisis, have paid little regard to the real economy as they look to shake-off the continued burden of toxic assets.

The German banking system has been criticised for its low profitability relative to other advanced economies. Based on their return on capital after tax this criticism seems fair.[66] This is not the place to debate the relative importance of bank profitability to an economy's success. What is interesting is the fact that the low profitability of the German banking sector cannot be blamed on the savings banks, indeed quite the opposite.

*Table 10: Profit for the financial year after tax as a percentage of the average capital as shown on the balance sheet*

|  | 1999 | 2000 | 2001 | 2002 | 2003 | 2004 |
|---|---|---|---|---|---|---|
| Regional and Other Commercial Banks | 10.08 | 7.41 | 1.26 | 6.62 | 2.25 | 2.16 |
| Large Commercial Banks | 5.48 | 7.23 | 5.69 | −3.30 | −11.99 | −3.56 |
| Sparkassen | 6.12 | 6.02 | 5.06 | 4.65 | 4.00 | 5.03 |
|  | 2005 | 2006 | 2007 | 2008 | 2009 | **Average** |
| Regional and Other Commercial Banks | 5.43 | 4.43 | 6.35 | 2.15 | −1.37 | **4.25** |
| Large Commercial Banks | 23.12 | 12.27 | 21.64 | −23.74 | −8.11 | **2.25** |
| Sparkassen | 5.60 | 4.95 | 4.21 | 2.12 | 4.43 | **4.74** |

Source: Deutsche Bundesbank, The performance of German credit institutions, September 2010

Table ten shows the return on capital of the regional commercial banks, large commercial banks and the Sparkassen. The Sparkassen are the most profitable banking group, and their profits are far more stable. It is interesting to note that the large commercial banks are less profitable than the other commercial banks, perhaps reflecting the fact that the large commercial banks engage in riskier activities resulting in more variable profits.

The success of the Swiss Cantonal banks and German Sparkassen suggests how we could reform the British banking market. We are in desperate need of greater competition and local banks provide a model worth emulating. The success of the Sparkassen and Cantonal banks also dispels any idea that local banks are necessarily unprofitable, inefficient or unstable.

# 4. Trustee Savings Banks

> It would be difficult, we fear, to convince either the people or their rulers that such an event is of far more importance and far more likely to increase the happiness and even the greatness of the nation than the most brilliant success of its arms or the most stupendous improvements of its trade or its agriculture – and yet we are persuaded that it is so.[67]
>
> H. O. Horne

So wrote the Edinburgh Review in 1815. The passage, taken from the comprehensive history of the Trustee Savings Banks by H. Oliver Horne, the first full-time Secretary to the Trustee Savings Bank Association, describes the spread of savings banks. Over the course of the 19th century, savings banks, or Trustee Savings Banks as they became known, spread across the country. They remained an important pillar of the British banking market until the 1980s.

Britain was not the first country to establish savings banks dedicated to serving the working classes. However, it was the first country to establish the savings bank as a formal, legally recognised institution when the Government drew up the Savings Bank Act of 1817.[68] It is sad and unfortunate that, despite achieving legal recognition and remaining a distinct part of British banking for over 150 years, the Government, with the support of some of the bank's trustees, though importantly not the vast majority of depositors, decided to controversially privatise them in 1986. It is also to be regretted that despite pioneering the savings bank model, Britain currently has one of the least diverse banking systems in the developed world. The loss of the savings banks, followed by the demutualisation of many building societies has resulted in a financial system that poorly serves customers and came to the brink of collapse during the recent financial crisis.

## *The origins and constitution of the Trustee Savings Banks*

At the beginning of the 19th century, savings banks began to spring up across Britain. These banks were set up by philanthropists who were keen to encourage greater saving amongst the growing working and lower-middle classes. Many were members of groups such as the Society for Bettering the Condition of the Poor and these philanthropists became 'trustees' of the banks and provided the necessary oversight and respect which would encourage depositors to place their small savings with them. Trustees were often members of the local aristocracy, members of parliament, rising industrialists or members of the church. Two factors were important: first, the trustee usually had a local presence and commanded respect as money was entrusted to them in the early years of the banks. Second, the trustee was required to commit time and (minimal) money; all trustees were unpaid and a minimal capital allocation was required to set a bank up.

The earliest banks began trading in the 1800s and, by the end of 1818, there were approximately 465 banks across the British Isles.[69] In England, Wales and Ireland alone, 132 banks were set up in 1818. Their growth has been described as 'one of the most rapid and spontaneous movements in our social history'.[70] The massive increase in the late 1810s can be partly attributed to the Savings Bank Act passed in 1817. Before the Act, which governed savings banks in England and Wales, it was unclear where responsibility within the banks lay. After the Act, the role of the trustees was defined, although the exact degree of their liability remained a contentious issue through the first half of the 19th century. Despite its limitations, the Act gave confidence to prospective founders that the banks they set up would be recognised by the Government. This resulted in the dramatic increase in the number of banks in 1818.

The Act acknowledged that trustees would oversee the banks and ensure that deposits were deposited with the Bank of England in return for a set rate of interest. Oversight by voluntary trustees and the placing of deposits with the Bank of England were two features of the savings banks that would remain until their dissolution in 1985.[71]

Similar to the Cantonal banks and the Sparkassen, the early British savings banks benefitted from local oversight of operations. Unlike Britain's current crop of large banks, the Trustee Savings Banks were set up to serve the needs of local depositors. The only downside to this was that there was little coordination between the banks until the late 19th century and cooperation between the banks was not formalised until early in the 20th century.

In 1891 the government passed an act that established an independent inspection committee to monitor the banks and ensure that each complied with professional auditing standards. This went some way to address the variable quality and professionalism of the banks. The larger, more profitable savings banks were seldom affected by financial failings; however the smaller banks sometimes fell prey to negligent or even fraudulent trustees. Experiments with different levels of trustee liability were trialled, yet until 1891 a solution could not be found because the government was unwilling to assume unlimited liability for the banks, and the banks were unwilling to be subject to government control. The 1891 Act created a measure of mutual oversight amongst the savings banks and in 1904 a further act made it easier for banks to amalgamate. This was a massive spur to consolidating the group, closing small banks through mergers with larger banks. The increase in branches allowed for economies of scale in terms of the products the banks offered and the service they were able to deliver. In 1919 there were 163 independent savings banks with 420 branches, by 1929 there were 113 banks but these banks had 466 branches between them.[72] 1929 also saw legislation that allowed customers to open accounts at more than one Trustee Savings Bank and made it easier for new banks to be set up. The result was that:

> The banks remained independent institutions relying for their success on local service and enterprise. But from this time their advance and general policy was to a far greater degree based on mutual agreements reached at meetings of the Trustee Savings Bank Association.[73]

This passage echoes one of the driving principles of the Swiss Cantonal banks to 'produce centrally, provide locally'.[74] In 1929 the Trustee Savings Banks became a group, with characteristics similar to those of the ASCB or Sparkassen-Finanzgruppe. The group was capable of benefitting from economies of scale and national coordination, but still retained a close link with local communities. In 1973 the Central Trustee Savings Bank was set up to provide banking and clearing services to all the banks in the group. A number of parliamentary acts passed from 1975 onwards permitted the Trustee Savings Banks to offer their customers a full range of financial services. As a result of recommendations made in the Government's Page Report of 1973 the Trustee Savings Banks reduced their number from 73 to 19 by 1976. The group of 19 banks were placed under the co-ordinating authority of the Trustee Savings Banks Central Board that led the development of the banks as they began to offer a wider range of financial services.[75] At this point they shared many of the same qualities, albeit in a far less sophisticated or developed sense, of the Cantonal banks and Sparkassen.

## *Trustee Savings Banks and local economies*

The Trustee Savings Banks were set up to provide more of the British population with the opportunity to save. They were not set up as a way of providing credit to local communities, and governments during the 19th century were concerned that investments by the banks had to be properly regulated to minimise the risk to depositors. Restrictions were also put in place because of the fear that the Trustee Savings Banks would begin to compete with the established commercial banks, something the commercial banks were keen to prevent. For this reason, it was decided in 1817 that all deposits had to be placed with the Bank of England. Furthermore, limits were placed on annual and total deposits to ensure that the banks did not gain market share from the commercial banks which served wealthier customers. Such restrictions were problematic: many depositors reached their deposit limit or wished to invest a certain portion of their savings in more lucrative investments. Furthermore, the banks themselves needed to attract larger deposits to cover their operating expenses. As the 19th century progressed, the larger banks looked for ways to respond to these problems, and it was the larger savings banks in Scotland that found innovative solutions that benefitted their local economies.

The Scottish Trustee Savings Banks were not brought under the same regulatory framework as the English banks until 1835. Until then the Scottish banks regularly invested their deposits in commercial banks, many of which provided a better interest rate than the Bank of England. Through this channel the Scottish banks helped the larger Scottish commercial banks increase their capital and resources. The real innovation however came in the mid-19th century when the Scottish banks led the way in opening Special Investment Departments (SIDs). The larger Scottish banks such as those in Edinburgh, Glasgow and Perth began to allow depositors who had reached their deposit limit to open accounts with the SIDs. The SIDs would invest deposits in local securities, mainly those secured on the taxes levied by local authorities. By 1891, when the SIDs began to be regulated, and their investments restricted, they accounted for 8.4 per cent of the total balances due to depositors in the savings banks across Britain.[76] In Scotland they made up 16.3 per cent.[77]

The SIDs invested in local economies by providing credit to local authorities to provide local services and improve local infrastructure. The records of the larger Scottish banks in 1890 detail the investments. The Dundee bank invested in the municipal gas, water and sewers commissioners, the school board and police commissioners. The Glasgow bank invested in similar securities as well as mortgages issued by the local authority. The Perth bank invested in bonds issued by Aberdeen town council.[78] Through such investments Trustee Savings Banks helped turn the deposits of local savers into productive investment for their local communities. Local knowledge was vital: the investments 'had been well chosen by the trustees of the banks, who knew the Local Authorities concerned'.[79]

An interesting contrast between the Trustee Savings Banks and the Cantonal and German savings banks is that the Trustee Savings Banks engaged in local lending against the regulatory wishes of the government. They were not mandated to invest in their local economies, but their local communities required investment and they were in the best position to provide it. When the government restricted the activities of the SIDs in 1891 and made it illegal for any new departments to open, the growth in SID deposits decreased dramatically.

Regulation by the government played an important part in the development of the SIDs. They grew dramatically before they were regulated in 1891, and then suffered a noticeable drop in investment until legislation passed in 1904 reinstated the freedom of investment they had previously enjoyed. Following this and only interrupted by the First World War the SIDs grew dramatically between 1905 and 1939.

One of the greatest, and little recognised, achievements of the Trustee Savings Banks was the way in which their success made redundant calls for more state-owned banks. Although the Post-Office savings bank was opened in 1861 and achieved great success, there was little attempt by governments in the late 19th and early 20th centuries to create state-owned banks to serve the rapidly growing towns and cities of Britain. The one counterexample was the Birmingham Municipal Bank that was set up in 1916 by Neville Chamberlain, then Lord Mayor of Birmingham. Chamberlain cited the lack of a Trustee Savings Bank in the city as the prime reason for his decision to set up the bank. He went on to tell a Trustee Savings Bank meeting in 1933 that had there been a Trustee Savings Bank in Birmingham, there would be no municipal bank.

*Table 11: Sums to depositors in the Special Investment Departments (£ sterling) (not adjusted for inflation)*

| Year | Sums to depositors in the Special Investment Departments |
|---|---|
| 1870 | 316,395 |
| 1875 | 1,098,589 |
| 1880 | 2,006,659 |
| 1885 | 3,318,593 |
| 1890 | 4,375,695 |
| 1895 | 4,744,019 |
| 1900 | 4,530,830 |
| 1905 | 5,590,784 |
| 1910 | 10,984,421 |
| 1913[80] | 14,361,041 |
| 1918 | 14,128,138 |
| 1925 | 27,038,323 |
| 1930 | 54,115,185 |
| 1935 | 89,822,401 |
| 1939[81] | 99,448,592 |

Source: H. O. Horne, *A History of Savings Banks*, 1947

Regulation had an important effect upon the development of the Trustee Savings Banks and the current Government needs to evaluate how regulation can be used to encourage competition and new-entrants in the British banking market.

## Government mishandling and the 'privatisation' of the Trustee Savings Banks

The demise, as well as the development, of the Trustee Savings Banks provides important lessons for the current Government. The Trustee Savings Banks were free to offer a wider range of financial services to customers in 1976 and simultaneously witnessed a period of consolidation as the group looked to improve its competitiveness. Nevertheless by 1984, as part of a wider programme of privatisation, the Government decided to 'privatise' the Trustee Savings Banks. The 'privatisation', the conversion of the Trustee Savings Banks into a privately-owned joint stock company, was complex and controversial because the banks were never publicly-owned in the usual sense.

At the time of the sale the Trustee Savings Bank Group included 16 banks with 1,650 branches. It was unclear in 1984 how the sale of the banks was to be conducted because of their 'peculiar' ownership rights, described at the time in the *Financial Times* as 'a banking scene riddle'.[82] The Government was keen to make it very clear that it did not own the banks and that the proceeds of the privatisation would not go to the exchequer but would be placed with the privatised bank. When the banks were sold, the assets of the Trustee Savings Banks Group were worth about £800 million and investors were offered 1.2 billion shares at 100p a share. As a result the total value of the assets of the Trustee Savings Banks Group was £2 billion and the new owners received not only the assets of the bank but also the proceeds of the sale.[83] It has been described as 'the give-away of the century'[84] and criticised by both advocates and opponents of privatisation.[85] The problems stemmed from the fact that no-one knew who rightly owned the Trustee Savings Banks.

The Government and the Trustee Savings Banks Central Board declared that the depositors had no claims on the bank and its surplus assets. This was challenged in the courts in both England and Scotland, and later for both cases in the House of Lords, where the case was finally settled in favour of the Trustee Savings Banks Central Board and the Government. The ruling in the Lords looked at section 1(3)(a) of the Trustee Savings Bank Act of 1981 which substantially reproduced the Savings Bank Act of 1817. Unfortunately the wording of this section of the Act does not make clear who owns the assets of the bank. Subparagraph three of section 1(3)(a) states that it is the job of the trustees 'to return the deposits and produce to the depositors'.[86] The two sides disagreed about the meaning of the word 'produce'. The depositors argued it meant that they owned the assets that their deposits had helped produce, that is the assets of the bank. In contrast the Government and the central board argued that produce simply meant interest, and the interest on their savings was all the depositors were owed. The Court decided that the central board's position was correct yet this seemed to run counter to further parts of the Act that identified the produce of the bank and the interests due on deposits as distinct.[87] Faced with such a contradiction, the two lords presiding over the two cases came to different conclusions. Lord Keith, perhaps prudently, did not explicitly rule on who owned the banks in his decision, choosing to just reject the claim that the depositors owned the banks. In contrast to this, Lord Templeman, argued that the state had owned the banks since the 1817 Act had instructed trustees to place funds with the Bank of England. Lord Templeman's decision embarrassed the Treasury that was keen to disown the banks.[88] Opponents of privatisation accused the Government of selling assets that were not theirs to sell; proponents of privatisation criticised the sale because it did not raise any public revenue and was mishandled. Both parties would have been happier if the legal status of the Trustee Savings Banks Group was clear, although this may have prevented the sale of the group if they were privately owned.

Failing to clear up who rightly owned the savings banks was one failure of the Government, the other was the way in which the flotation and subsequent development of the Trustee Savings Banks was handled. The privatisation of the Trustee Savings Banks saw the group sold at a significant discount. The newly privatised entity did not respond to the needs of shareholders, many of them previous customers and staff, and quickly made disastrous business decisions. The Government, and the professional financiers hired to execute the sale, found it difficult to accurately assess the worth of the group. While it was relatively easy to value the assets of the Trustee Savings Banks Group, it was difficult to assess the value of the new entity which would also include the proceeds of the sale. The cash raised in the sale would be returned to the business and how this cash was spent would determine the true price of the new bank's shares. Those in the City of London were concerned that the Trustee Savings Banks Central Board, with little experience of acquisitions, would spend the proceeds of the sale unwisely. This view coloured market perception and the price at which the shares would have to be sold. This uncertainty, however, also meant that there was an opportunity for shareholders to buy what could be a significantly undervalued company. This opportunity was summed up by the *Financial Times* in 1986 when it advised investors: 'Best to exploit markets rather than argue with them.'[89]

Those who feared that the Trustee Savings Banks sale would result in the group being undervalued were proved right. On the first day of public trading of the 50p partly paid shares,[90] the share price opened at 100p and later fell back to 85.5p.[91]

Fears about the ability of the Trustee Savings Banks to spend the proceeds of privatisation prudently proved well-founded. After privatisation the new Trustee Savings Bank Group plc significantly altered its business model. Local customers were no longer important as the Trustee Savings Bank Central Board looked to challenge the incumbent commercial banks by serving wealthier customers and offering a wide array of services, including merchant banking. The new Trustee Savings Bank Group plc acquired Target Group, a provider of life insurance, unit trusts and pensions, and Hill Samuel, a merchant bank, soon after flotation. Many shareholders were concerned about this new direction: at one of the Annual General Meetings of the Trustee Savings Bank Group shortly after privatisation, there was 'violent opposition to the proposed take-over of the merchant bank Hill Samuel'.[92] Unfortunately these concerns were ignored as the new owners ruled that a no-confidence motion bought by the shareholders was contrary to the articles of association of the new entity. The shareholders were proved right as the group rued both decisions, and its failure to sensibly invest the proceeds of privatisation led to it suffering a loss of £248 million in 1987 and a loss of £47 million in 1991. This prompted a rethink of the group's strategy as it divested itself of 18 businesses between 1991 and 1993.

The privatisation and subsequent development of the Trustee Savings Bank Group plc was a debacle and it provides a couple of important lessons for the current Government. First is the need to ensure that new banks operate under assured legal conditions. New local banks will need to be free from political wrangling and should stand as independent institutions, otherwise customers will have little confidence in them. As well as being clearly defined by law, mutuals, cooperatives, or banks where the trustees oversee operations should not be placed at a disadvantage in relation to joint-stock businesses. Secondly, the Government must constantly assess developments in the banking market, especially the effects of any decision it takes. The privatisation of the Trustee Savings Banks did not improve choice, competition or outcomes for consumers and the Government must shoulder some of the blame for this. As the current Government encourages reform of the British banking market, it needs to recognise that its decisions can have an enormous impact. Reform of the regulatory system, removing the *de facto* state subsidy for large banks (discussed in more detail in chapter seven) and the public sale of the Lloyds Banking Group branches and Northern Rock: these are all actions that the Government should take, or should have taken, with an eye to improving competition and improving outcomes for businesses and customers.

Sadly the sale of part of the Lloyds Banking Group created the worrying precedent that takeover bids by new banks will be financially discriminated against. In 2011 the Financial Services Authority decided to penalise a new bank, NBNK, that was bidding for the Lloyds assets by making it clear that Lloyds would have to inject an additional £1.1 billion in capital as part of a sale to NBNK. It would not have to inject this additional capital if the bank was sold to another bidder, the Co-operative bank, despite the fact that both bidders offered £1.5 billion for the assets.[93]

Despite this failure, the Government still has the opportunity to overhaul the regulatory structure, an opportunity it must not waste. Importantly a revised regulatory framework, discussed in greater detail in chapter seven, should encourage competition; this will give locally-oriented banks the chance to flourish again.

# 5. Localised banking today: The Airdrie Savings Bank and Handelsbanken

The Trustee Savings Banks may give an anachronistic impression of local banks yet the Airdrie Savings Bank and Handelsbanken, a Swedish bank, are contemporary examples of banks whose primary aim is to serve the local community. Both have expanded during the financial crisis, offering customers security and a level of service not provided by Britain's large banks.

## *The origins and constitution of the Airdrie Savings Bank*

The Airdrie Savings Bank was established in 1835 and operates under the Scottish Savings Bank Act of 1819. It was the only Trustee Savings Bank that refused to join the consolidated group that developed after 1975 and as a result is the only remaining independent Trustee Savings Bank. The Bank has eight branches, 103 employees[94] and serves approximately 60,000 customers in the central belt of Scotland.[95]

Like the original Trustee Savings Banks, the Airdrie Savings Bank is overseen by the Board of Trustees with further oversight provided by committees on auditing, remuneration and nominations. The eleven trustees are predominantly local business people. The trustees are self-selected and positions on the Board are decided at the Annual General Meeting of the bank. The trustees are 'appointed to represent the interests of depositors' and do so by monitoring customer feedback.[96] Their formal duties include:

- Preparing annual financial statements;
- keeping up-to-date accounting records;
- reviewing capital adequacy and liquidity provision;
- providing a monthly review of financial information;
- and reviewing and updating the bank's strategic plan on an annual basis.[97]

The trustees receive no remuneration for their work, and the staff, including the management, took a pay cut in 2010 despite the bank recording a profit.[87]

Constituted under the 1819 Scottish Savings Banks Act the Airdrie Savings Bank is not a full mutual, but has mutual characteristics. It is run in the interests of customers and has no investors. However the customers, unlike members of a mutual, cannot claim any ownership of the bank. As a result, the position of customers is unclear. The 1819 Act states that the bank is responsible for 'returning the whole or any part of such deposit, and the produce thereof' to the customer.[99] A similar instruction governed the Trustee Savings Banks and during their privatisation the question of ownership revolved around the concept of 'produce' (as outlined in chapter four). The Airdrie Savings Bank follows the precedent set by the decision in that case, namely that customers are entitled to the interest on their deposits but not the assets of the bank. The trustees are responsible for the operation of the bank and if the bank were to fail or to be sold, the courts would have to decide whether any surplus would go to depositors or the British Treasury. As a result the Airdrie Savings Bank could be subject to similar legal disputes as the Trustee Savings Banks if sold. The precedent of that case does indicate that the trustees have a right to sell the bank if they see fit. This could be a concern for customers if trustees do not seem committed to keeping the bank in its current form, although there is no indication that this is likely to happen. Nevertheless, this distinguishes the Airdrie Savings Bank from the Sparkassen which have their operating structure protected in the Federal and Länder constitutions.

## *Small but successful*

Despite the difficult financial situation, the Airdrie Savings Bank has been immensely successful in the last few years. It was reported last year that prominent Scottish business leaders were 'investing' in the bank[100] by placing deposits with the bank and applying for loans, and there is talk of it opening up a ninth branch in the near future.[101] The bank offers savings, current and investment accounts, overdrafts, personal and business loans and mortgages. Loans are funded from deposits; the bank receives no wholesale funding and four-fifths of loans go to local businesses.[102] Of these loans and mortgages, 35 per cent have a maturity of five years or more and 19 per cent a maturity of between one and five years.[103] Long-term loans provide an important source of reliable credit for local businesses and households.

In the period after 1975, when the bank refused to join the Trustee Savings Bank group, it did not have any customer loans. From this point, it prudently increased its loan volume, setting aside retained earnings as reserves, investing in UK Government bonds and other fixed interest securities and maintaining deposits with other banks for day-to-day liquidity. The bank was forced to be prudent because it is unable to issue shares to increase the capital of the bank. Until recently the bank operated a policy whereby approximately one-third of customer deposits were lent out, a third were deposited with other banks for short-term liquidity purposes and a third were invested in government bonds.[104] However this situation is changing as the bank expands and responds to recent reforms where deposits with other banks no longer count as liquidity for regulatory purposes. The result is that the bank is now moving towards a situation where 50 per cent of its deposits are used for loans, 37.5 per cent are placed in gilts and 12.5 per cent are funds held on deposit with other banks for day-to-day operations. As of 31 October 2010, the bank had capital of £15 million covering assets of £146.1 million resulting in a tier 1 capital ratio of 10.2 per cent, far higher than the large British banks had before the recent crisis despite having the advantage of being able to issue shares to increase their capital ratio.

Branch staff are responsible for decisions that affect local customers. Loan decisions are made with little use of credit scoring: staff of the bank assess the ability of potential borrowers to pay the money back. As a result of good knowledge of local businesses and economic conditions, bad debts were just 1.7 per cent of the total lending volumes in 2010, £101,000 of £36,051,000 worth of loans. The percentage of bad debts was also kept relatively low and constant during the financial crisis, despite a steady increase in loans since 2008.

*Table 12: Airdrie Savings Bank five year financial summary (£ thousands)*

|  | 2006 | 2007 | 2008 | 2009 | 2010 |
|---|---|---|---|---|---|
| Loans and advances to customers | 28,072 | 33,475 | 25,526 | 29,163 | 36,051 |
| Customer accounts | 111,596 | 114,896 | 124,927 | 123,932 | 130,566 |
| Profit after taxation | 505 | 456 | 569 | 114 | 326 |

Source: Airdrie Savings Bank, Annual Report and Accounts 2010

As with the Sparkassen and Swiss Cantonal banks, the Airdrie Savings Bank has seen its customer deposits increase during the period of the financial crisis. Its safety and stability makes it an attractive alternative to the embattled large commercial banks, although this attraction is somewhat mitigated by the fact that all British banks benefit from an equal level of deposit insurance. The Airdrie Savings Bank managed to increase lending during the crisis, although not as dramatically as the German and Swiss banks. Despite a dip in 2008, current lending levels are above those registered before the crisis. The Bank also managed to stay profitable throughout the crisis. Profits are ploughed back into the bank to increase reserves or lending with only a minimal across-the-board bonus paid to all staff when conditions permit. As a result of its lending policies and reinvestment of profits, the Airdrie Savings Bank is exceptionally well capitalised.

Refusing to join the Trustee Savings Bank group in the period of consolidation that followed the Trustee Savings Banks Act of 1975 the Airdrie Savings Bank managed to avoid the controversies over its ownership that plagued the Trustee Savings Banks as they faced privatisation. With its independence guaranteed the bank has been successful in serving businesses and individuals in the central belt of Scotland. The challenge for new or small banks is to expand and take advantage of the failings of the incumbent banks. Challenging the dominant players in any industry would be an uphill struggle and this is made all the more difficult by the fact that the barriers to greater competition in the banking sector are somewhat unique. The next chapter describes these barriers and what steps the Government needs to take if the unique failings of the British banking market are to be addressed.

## Handelsbanken: A Swedish relationship bank in Britain

Svenska Handelsbanken, or just Handelsbanken as it is known in the UK, is a public limited company that offers banking services and operates in twenty two countries. Nevertheless it operates in much the same way as the local banks discussed in this report. Each branch must limit its operations to a particular area, encouraging them to focus on serving their local community. When Handelsbanken began to significantly increase its UK operations in the early 2000s, it continued to employ the branch-led business model that had been so successful in Sweden: Handelsbanken gives branches the freedom to decide on pricing and the interest offered to savers, the wages of staff, the majority of marketing campaigns and, most importantly, the majority of credit decisions. 57 per cent of loan decisions are made entirely at the branch level.[105] This figure is far more impressive when one bears in mind the fact that no decision on credit can be taken without the branch's approval.

In the 1970's Handelsbanken reformed its business model and devolved responsibility to the branch level. Since then the bank has enjoyed enormous success. Handelsbanken prospered through the Swedish financial crisis of the early 1990s and, during the recent financial crisis, the bank expanded its British operations dramatically. Since the end of 2009 the bank has increased the number of UK branches by 89 per cent and now has 117 branches in Great Britain.[106] Compare this to the 70 or so branches of Northern Rock that were recently sold to Virgin Money and it is clear that Handelsbanken is an important, if still relatively small, bank in the UK.

Handelsbanken outperformed the large British banks in 2010. Handelsbanken had a return on equity of 12.9 per cent in 2010 compared to 7.2 per cent for Barclays and 9.5 per cent for HSBC. Handelsbanken's cost to income ratio was 54.4 per cent for its British banks: Barclays, RBS, Lloyds and HSBC had cost to income ratios of 64 per cent, 59.9 per cent, 46.6 per cent and 55.2 per cent respectively.[107] More importantly Handelsbanken continued to lend to British businesses during the crisis:

*Table 13: Capital ratio of the Handelsbanken group and lending volumes in the UK (£ millions)*

|  | Q3 2008 | Q3 2009 | Q3 2010 | Q3 2011 |
|---|---|---|---|---|
| Capital ratio (%) | 15.2 | 16.7 | 20.7 | 19.0 |
| Loans to corporates in the UK | 4,065 | 4,461 | 4,863 | 5,900 |
| Loans to households in the UK | 848 | 1,057 | 1,366 | 2,029 |

Source: Handelsbanken, Factbook 2009 Q1, 2010 Q1, 2011 Q3 2011

Handelsbanken increased its capital ratio from 15.2 per cent in September 2008 to 19 per cent in September 2011.[108] At the same time as it increased its capital, the bank continued to lend. Lending to households and corporates in the UK has grown by 45 per cent over the last three years despite the insecure economic outlook.

Although Handelsbanken differs markedly to the large British banks in its approach to banking, it, like them, is a public limited company with shareholders. How was Handelsbanken able to resist shareholder pressure during the boom years and continue to operate a relationship-banking business when its competitors were pursuing quick and easy profits? Part of the answer lies with the shareholder structure of Handelsbanken. 20.8 per cent of the bank's share capital is held equally by two bodies, one is an investment company set up by the bank in 1944, and the other is a profit sharing mutual that all employees have an equal stake in.[109] Undoubtedly these two shareholders exert a significant amount of influence over the bank, but this is not the only reason that Handelsbanken pursues a locally-oriented relationship-banking model. The fact that Handelsbanken outperforms its rivals and achieves an impressive return on equity means that shareholders are rewarded for investing in the bank; such success limits shareholder pressure for reform.

Handelsbanken's success, the recent acquisition of part of Lloyds Banking Group by the Co-operative Bank[110] and the emergence of Metro Bank, the first new UK high-street bank for more than one hundred years, all indicate that the British banking market may be opening up to greater competition. Nevertheless, limited success should not lull politicians and those interested in creating a better British banking system into complacency. There are still a number of crippling problems that new banks face. The first set of problems is the many barriers to entry, some of which are particularly problematic for non-shareholder banks. The second problem is the cost of setting up a bank. The Government can solve the first problem and take steps to mitigate the second. Finally, the Government needs to address the issue of diversity in the British banking market. Thanks to the wave of demutualisations and the sale of the Trustee Savings Banks, Britain does not have the variety of banks that Switzerland and Germany are blessed with. To address this issue, the Government must take steps to create the correct legal structure that can create a secure environment for the growth of local banks.

# 6. The barriers to British local banks

Airdrie Savings Bank is a good example of what can be achieved by a local bank with a cautious yet profitable business model. Nevertheless, it is only one bank with eight branches. Critics may argue that similar institutions will never achieve sufficient scale to challenge Britain's dominant commercial banks. Undoubtedly one needs to be realistic. It would be foolish to suggest that a single local bank or centralised network of local banks, similar to the Trustee Savings Banks, could capture significant market share from the dominant incumbent banks in the near future. Nevertheless, opening up the British banking market to more competition would erode the stranglehold the current institutions have over the British credit market, and over time a far more competitive market would emerge. Henry Angest, Chairman of Arbuthnot Banking Group, and Atholl Turrell, Vice-Chairman of Arbuthnot Securities, are confident that new banks could emerge to challenge the dominant players: 'There is no shortage of entrepreneurs ready to create such small banks.'[111]

The Government has been called upon to intervene in the banking market to provide funding to businesses directly. Such intervention is necessary at present, and could be extremely beneficial and necessary in the future if market failures remain and marginalised groups or businesses struggle to access appropriately priced credit. However, an enduring solution would be one that creates the foundations for a successful banking system. While the immediate priority for the Government may be to ensure that credit-starved British businesses are supplied with funding, removing the significant entry barriers that new banks face will lay the foundations for a better British banking system in the long-run. This section describes some of the hurdles and challenges that new entrants face.

Much of this section discusses the regulatory system and the Financial Services Authority (FSA). At present, the Government plans to have a new regulatory structure in place by the end of 2012, when the Financial Conduct Authority (FCA) will take over from the FSA. There is little indication that the Government is examining how the regulatory changes will address the barriers to entry that new banks face. This is despite the fact that the reforms present a unique opportunity to tackle the problems outlined below. At present, the FCA will take over from the FSA in assessing prospective banks and it is likely that the FCA will be just as ineffective as the FSA at the task.

## Completing the FSA application

In his response to the Treasury Select Committee on the ICB's Final Report, the Rt Hon George Osborne MP, Chancellor of the Exchequer, stated: 'I want the process of getting a banking licence to be as quick and as straightforward as possible.'[112]

Unfortunately the current process is far from straightforward and is a serious barrier to entry for new banks. All banks need to obtain a licence from the FSA before they can begin business. The FSA currently states that it will attempt to assess and give a regulatory decision on a new bank in six months if the bank submits a 'complete' application. The FSA also promises to process an 'incomplete' application in twelve months.[113] What is not stated is that if a bank's application is deemed incomplete after twelve months then the bank will be failed and forced to reapply, starting the twelve month time limit again. New banks need to know when they will be required to have the bank ready for FSA testing as they need to give certainty to investors. It is welcome that the FSA commits to processing the application in six months, however this period does not start until an application is deemed complete and the FSA decides what a 'complete' application is. It can request further information and possibly additional funds at any time, thus delaying the process indefinitely.

The six-month promise is useless because investors cannot be told when to expect this six-month period to begin. Furthermore, banks cannot accurately plan when the bank will need to be built so that the FSA can begin testing. The result is that new banks and their investors are confronted with significant uncertainty from the outset.

## *Achieving regulatory approval*

The FSA examines the business plan of a prospective bank and can suggest alterations or indicate where specific business decisions will affect how the bank is regulated. Such an examination is necessary if the FSA is to properly assess new banks. The problem is that the FSA appears to penalise banks that fail to conform to the standard model it endorses. This stifles innovation and disproportionally affects new banks that seek to use different business models and techniques to challenge incumbent firms.

The FSA has a clear preference for banks with a 'high street' presence; it looks more favourably upon new banks that propose to open branches.[114] If an entrant wishes to serve customers remotely, through internet and telephone banking, it also prefers it if the bank plans to open branches that remote banking customers can reach if needed. The FSA's preference for this 'high street' presence discriminates against new entrants that do not have the necessary capital to fund a significant number of branches. It also stifles innovation with banks dissuaded from looking to serve customers at a lower cost, and often far more efficiently, through remote channels such as online, through the telephone, or through a mobile application.

The FSA's preference for familiarity also extends to the staff and the owners of banks. The FSA is significantly less likely to block or obstruct an application if it is submitted by an applicant it knows or if the new bank plans to employ senior executives that have extensive experience working in one of Britain's large banks. John Kay described this problem when giving evidence to the Treasury Committee as part of the Independent Commission on Banking:

> If you want to have a licence for a new bank, not only is it hard work, but in order to do it, you have to promise to behave like an existing bank and recruit the people around existing banks in order to operate it for you.[115]

The need to 'recruit the people around existing banks' creates the odd situation whereby a new entrant has to employ executives and employees that have worked within established institutions and within orthodox business models to implement what could be an innovative banking service. This is not to suggest that experience in the industry is not beneficial for those looking to start a bank, but preventing investors, executives and business people from outside the world of banking entering the industry robs it of an important source of innovation.

A preference for experienced owners and executives is problematic enough, but there are even reports of the FSA refusing to help inexperienced entrepreneurs. The Rt Hon Andrew Stephenson, the Conservative Member of Parliament for Pendle, in a recent parliamentary debate on manufacturing stated:

> In Pendle a local businessman called David Fishwick is trying to do exactly what my hon. Friend suggests. He is trying to create his own bank to help small and medium-sized enterprises in Pendle and Burnley. The regulations are so detailed and engrossing that the FSA has refused to help him, despite his instructing high-flying lawyers. So far, it has even refused to meet him to discuss the creation of a bank that would directly help small and medium-sized manufacturers in Pendle and Burnley.[116]

The businessman mentioned is currently in the process of trying to set up his bank and Channel 4 is filming his efforts for a television show.[117] His experience highlights the commonly mentioned problem that the FSA is extremely risk-averse, conservative, and does very little to support new entrants or encourage competition. At present, the FSA is tasked with providing both advice and oversight of new financial institutions and does neither satisfactorily. The advisory and regulatory functions would be better carried out by separate institutions.

## *Meeting capital requirements*

A bank's capital reserves are used to protect it against possible losses that may occur on its loans or investments. A bank must also hold liquid assets, such as cash that can be used at short notice if it needs to pay depositors or cover other liabilities the bank may have. Both are important safeguards that all banks need. However, the current capital and liquidity rules significantly discriminate against new or 'unorthodox' banks.

The capital requirements for banks are set internationally by the Bank of International Settlements in the Basel Accords.[118] The FSA enforces these accords which have been transposed into EU regulations in the Capital Requirements Directives (CRDs). The FSA must adhere to international standards but can set rules where the Basel Accords and the CRDs are not specific. As a result, the FSA currently forces UK banks to keep capital reserves of 8.5 per cent. This is calculated as a percentage of the sum of the bank's assets: its loans and investments. Capital reserves of 8.5 per cent are only permitted if the bank internally risk-weights its assets. More capital must be held to cover riskier assets such as unsecured overdrafts; less risky assets such as mortgages (secured on the value of the house) require less capital. 'Advanced internal risk-weighting' by large banks can help reduce their reserve requirement to 8.5 per cent, however new banks are unable to do this because they lack the sophisticated risk managements systems and are not examined by the ratings agencies that scrutinise a bank's risk-weighting. As a result of this, new banks have to hold more capital.

The FSA calculates the amount of capital that a new bank is required to hold by examining the expected balance sheet for the bank's fifth year of operation. The result of this is that new banks may be expected to hold capital reserves equal to 100 per cent or more of their assets in the first year of trading. When, or if, the bank reaches its fifth year of trading then its capital requirement may constitute 10 per cent of its assets, but until this happens, a new bank is forced to hold far more capital than an old bank, impairing its ability to compete.

These capital rules also deter possible investors, who are forced to buy a significant number of shares to ensure that the bank has the required capital. As a result, an investor is forced to make a big commitment coupled with the fact that they will also have to wait a significant time before they see a return on their investment

The rules on capital reserves are a significant barrier to entry for new banks. Despite the fact that new banks are generally easier to regulate, because they tend to focus on retail services and process simple transactions, they are forced to hold crippling levels of capital. Undoubtedly, a new bank, like any new business, is more likely to fail than an established firm, however the risk to the financial system and the British tax payer is minute when compared to the money used to bail-out many banks during the financial crisis.

## *Meeting liquidity requirements*

The rules on liquidity penalise new entrants. For small banks and building societies the FSA has created a simplified regime where it sets liquidity ratios based on the types of deposits held. The FSA makes the distinction between 'lower quality' and 'higher quality' deposits. Lower quality deposits are:

- Those that are acquired quickly when a bank manages to attract savers;
- large deposits that exceed the level of deposit insurance (currently £85,000 per person);
- deposits in online-only accounts.[118]

All other deposits are classed as 'higher quality'.[120] The FSA estimates that lower quality deposits could experience outflows of 20 per cent and a bank is required to hold liquid assets that could cover such an outflow. It also estimates that higher quality deposits could experience outflows of 10 per cent. A study by Deloitte illustrates the effect of these rules. A £500,000 mortgage, that is due to be paid back after at least a year, can be funded by £588,235 of higher quality deposits or £714,286 of lower quality deposits.[121]

These rules penalise new banks. New entrants will hopefully attract deposits quickly as they gain market share. New banks are also more likely to have a disproportionate amount of large deposits that are placed in the bank by its investors. As they lack an extensive branch network new entrants are also more likely to attract customers with online deposits. The result is that the rules look almost tailored to deter prospective banks. Like the rules on capital, they are an excessive way to mitigate risk which damages competition.

There is little reason to think, and little evidence that supports the idea that online deposits are more likely to be withdrawn. The same goes for new deposits: there is even the possibility that new depositors are less likely to leave as they have just undertaken the inconvenient step of changing banks.

Clearly the solution to the problems posed by the liquidity and capital rules is to allow new banks to build up liquidity and capital as they grow, in much the same way that the Airdrie Savings Bank did when it began to offer more services after 1985. It is entirely feasible that the regulator could monitor a bank's growth and force it to hold more capital and liquid assets as it takes on more customers and poses more of a risk to savers and the taxpayer.

## Accessing the payment systems

Banks need to access the payment systems that allow for money to be transferred between different institutions. The clearing systems that process BACS (previously Bankers' Automated Clearing Services), CHAPS (Clearing House Automated Payment System), Faster Payments, ATMs, Cheques, Direct Debits, Direct Credits, and the Link Scheme are all run and owned by the large established banks through VocaLink Holdings Limited. The members of VocaLink Holdings can access the payment systems directly through a settlement account with the Bank of England. New banks, by definition, cannot meet the necessary criteria for directly joining these systems and so must gain access to a settlement account through a sort code issued by an 'agency bank'. In effect, new banks access the payment infrastructure through one of the incumbent banks at a price set by that bank.

Banks set prices for new banks when processing transactions: the price per transaction falls as the number of transactions increases. Britain's large banks dominate the agency market and the prices set by different banks do not differ significantly. The real problem however is the opaque nature of the system, new banks are forced into agency agreements yet have little idea how much direct access would cost; they are forced to accept what the big banks give them.

It is perhaps hard to imagine a more effective way of enshrining a monopoly than by allowing incumbent firms to set the price of market access for those wishing to challenge them.

One of the reasons given for not allowing new banks direct access is that they pose a risk to the clearing systems because for many systems, including CHAPS and BACS, transactions are processed in batches and there is a risk that new banks will not have the necessary funds to process all transactions. Were this to occur, the system would be disrupted. However with the roll-out of the Faster Payments system, transactions are processed in 2 hours and there is far less risk that transactions will not be completed due to a significant number being processed at once. Britain's big banks have been slow to roll-out Faster Payments systems across all their accounts. If the regulator were to force complete take-up of this system, then new banks could access the payment systems directly.

Forcing the adoption of the Faster Payments system is one change the Government could make to help new banks. More importantly, the governance of the payment systems needs to be drastically reformed to allow all banks equal access and an equal voice in the running of the systems. The payment systems need to take the interests of new entrants into account; currently new banks have to wait until they receive their licence from the FSA before they can test their payment systems. This adds another three months onto the already protracted process of setting up the bank, further frustrating potential investors. The reformed payment systems would agree to test new banks when they wished and as quickly as possible.

## Increasing market share

A new bank needs to compete with incumbent market players to attract customers. A serious disadvantage for any small bank, and so something that, in all likelihood, will affect new banks, is that they will suffer a loss if they attempt to offer 'free' current accounts. It is estimated that a bank needs a market share of 10 per cent before they can offer free accounts without a loss.[122]

No current account is free. It costs to maintain them and the low-balances in many current accounts do not compensate for this. 'Free' accounts are paid for through charges and the money that banks make when other banks use their ATMs. An ATM withdrawal costs approximately 27p and balance enquiries cost approximately 14p.[123] Banks with large market shares and lots of ATMs benefit at the expense of those with few ATMs. This is because banks with few ATMs will have to pay other banks when their customers use ATMs other than their own. This also applies to MasterCard and Visa services. Banks profit every time a customer of another bank pays a merchant that banks with them. The result of both systems is that small banks are at a disadvantage.

There is no simple solution to this problem and economies of scale exist in many industries. Small banks could share a common bank infrastructure as many credit unions in America do. The government could also put public infrastructure, such as the Post Office, at the disposal of small banks. The Government should also look more closely at the use of shared branches for all banks, not just credit unions. These shared branches would need to be available to all banks and could be jointly funded by participating institutions, they would help maintain branch facilities in underserved areas.[124] These possible solutions suggest that the problems of scale could be overcome or mitigated.

## *Regulating diversity*

One of the overriding problems alluded to above is the 'one size fits all' regulatory regime. New banks, small banks or those with different governance models than that of the large shareholder banks that dominate the market, are forced to meet unsuitable regulatory requirements. This view is shared by Henry Angest, Chairman of Arbuthnot Banking Group and Atholl Turrell, Vice-Chairman of Arbuthnot Securities:

> This "one size fits all" approach to regulation saddles prospective new entrants with unnecessarily onerous capital requirements and high ongoing costs relating to compliance and governance, and leads to interminable delays in securing licences, launching products and hiring staff.[125]

This is particularly clear in a number of different areas. The Financial Services Compensation Scheme operates as a mutual insurance system whereby banks pay to compensate customers that are affected by the failure of another bank. There is no problem with this in principle, but it operates as if all banks present a similar amount of risk to customers. This is clearly not the case in the British market; the operations of some banks are far more risky and the fallout from their failure far more damaging than that of other banks. The scheme needs to be reformed so that the payments banks make reflect the risk that they pose to their customers and the financial system.

The capital and liquidity requirements discussed above are another case in point. The current regulations, a substantial part of which are set internationally, need to be implemented in a way that encourages and safeguards diversity in the British banking market. An important concern at present is that the Basel III rules, that must be fully implemented in Europe by 2021, pose peculiar problems to mutuals. A report by Deloitte surveyed British building societies and concluded that the vast majority of those surveyed had already met the Basel III capital requirements but that the 'building society sector will need to continue to look for alternative ways of raising permanent capital and long-term liquidity'.[126] Under Basel III banks and building societies will have to increase their tier 1 capital from 2 per cent to a possible 9.5 per cent. Tier 1 capital must be equity (shares), retained earnings or a similar asset able to absorb losses. Tier 1 capital can absorb losses because shareholders are not entitled to be paid in full (shares can fall in value) and retained earnings are the banks to use as it sees fit. The problem for building societies is that they cannot raise equity because they do not issue shares. The challenge is to find an asset that can absorb losses but which does not destroy the mutual governance structure whereby customers, not shareholders, own the building society.

The Basel rules pose a problem for established mutuals, but they pose an even greater challenge to prospective firms looking to enter the market. New mutuals will find raising capital even more difficult without the advantage of the strong capital base enjoyed by the established mutuals. The worry is that the regulatory reforms will stifle variety in the financial sector. If mutuals find it far harder to meet the capital requirements, then entrepreneurs will shun this form of bank or building society and instead generate investment through a public limited company. This could have serious consequences for local banks that may wish to channel local savings into loans and investments without serving shareholders. The majority of the local savings banks that have been examined, with the exception of some of the Swiss Cantonal banks and Svenska Handelsbanken do not have any form of equity capital.

Representatives of savings banks and cooperatives are rightly concerned about the Basel III rules. Karl-Heinz Boos, managing-director of the Association of German Public Sector Banks (VOEB) stated:

> The agreement is a regulatory shot in the dark as no studies on the impact are envisaged. We see the danger that the ability of German banks to supply loans to the economy will be significantly curtailed. Small and mid-sized companies that have no access to capital markets will suffer in particular. It seems the timetable here was more important than quality (making this) [the Basel III rules] a compromise package with risks and side effects. [127]

His fears were echoed by Gerhard Hoffman of the Central Organisation of the German Cooperative Banks (BVR):

> Business models with little risks are burdened in the same way as business models with high risks. Additionally, not all problems can be solved with more equity.[128]

Basel III will be implemented in the UK through transposing the European Union's Capital Requirements Directive (CRD) IV into British law. The exact form the CRD takes will be decided by negotiations in Europe. The British Government needs to make sure that the CRD IV does not present significant problems for mutuals, especially new mutuals. The Government should push for lower capital and liquidity requirements for new entrants and also ensure that new mutuals are not discriminated against by being unable to issue shares. It is overwhelmingly important that future regulations do not discriminate against certain types of banks, in this case mutuals and savings banks that do not have shareholders.

Safeguarding variety in the financial system requires a regulator that values and encourages it. In the future, the FSA or its successor, the Financial Conduct Authority (FCA), will need to do more in this regard. At present the FSA favours new bank applicants that propose to develop a 'high street' presence. They are wary of online or telephone banking operation and impose higher liquidity requirements on them. There is an inclination to favour applicants that plan to employ familiar executives, particularly those with experience in the dominant British banks, or those with direct experience of banking. In some extreme cases (such as that described by the Rt Hon Andrew Stephenson above) there have been reports of the FSA refusing to meet applicants that do not fit this profile. As it reforms the regulatory system the Government must ensure that the regulator does not carry on these discriminatory practices. New or 'unorthodox' banks should not be viewed with greater suspicion by the FSA or FCA. The application process needs to set clear requirements that all banks must meet.

There may be some risks that accompany diversity, new business models may fail and banks may go under. Fortunately, these banks are likely to be small. The regulator would do well to listen to David Potter, former deputy chairman of Investec Bank UK:

> What the regulators need to understand is that these new banks will be too small to be systemic and thus do not need to be regulated in the same way as the (as yet unbundled) clearers.[129]

Failure is necessary if innovation is to occur. Without innovation, banking will be far more inefficient and far less secure than it is now.

# 7. Conclusion: British local banks

Impressive as the successes of the Swiss Cantonal banks, the Sparkassen and Airdrie Savings Bank are, for more British local banks to emerge and flourish, government action is needed. This chapter describes four important steps the Government should take:

1. The Government should remove the barriers to entry in banking.
2. The Government needs to create a new legal structure governing local banks.
3. The Government should help local authorities and private individuals to set up local banks.
4. The Government needs to encourage cooperation between local banks and other financial institutions such as credit unions and community development finance institutions (CDFIs).

*Removing the barriers to entry in banking*

The first step the Government needs to take is to remove the significant barriers to entry that prospective banks face.

- The Government should reform the payments systems. It should end the position of power that the large banks currently hold by forcing equal access and equal ownership of the systems. All new banks that meet the necessary regulatory requirements and wish to access the systems directly should be allowed to. To this end, the Government must disband VocaLink Holdings Limited and ensure that a body, owned by its members and run fairly, controls the systems. The Government should also disband the Payments Council and reconstitute it with all members having equal power.

- The Government should ensure that the current reforms to the switching process, the result of which will see credits and debits and current accounts switched in seven days, are implemented as soon as possible. The current deadline is September 2013 but this could be brought forward to January 2013.

The Government needs to reform the regulatory system for new banks. The current plan is that the Financial Conduct Authority (FCA) will take over the majority of the FSA's duties, including the assessment of prospective banks. Without reform it is likely that the FCA will simply become the FSA reincarnate and banks will face the same problems that they do now. This cannot be allowed to happen. The FCA, or perhaps even a separate regulator, needs to be able to handle new banks.

- The application process should be simplified so that prospective banks are given a clear time frame in which their application will be processed if they submit the necessary information. The regulator should not delay processing an application by requesting additional information or funding that is not made clear at the start. A clear application process will help new banks generate the necessary investment.

- The FCA or a separate regulator responsible for prospective banks should have no preference for 'known' executives or business models. Online banks should not be discriminated against and nor should entrepreneurs with little previous experience in banking.

- The Government needs to create a new body that will provide advice to prospective banks. At present the FSA provides advice but this often means that it does not provide prospective banks with clear information on what is required of them when making an application. The new regulatory framework should include an advisory body and a regulatory body. The two institutions should be separate.

- The liquidity and capital requirements for new banks should be phased in over time. Discriminatory liquidity rules that penalise online or new deposits should be scrapped. Capital rules that could discourage banks without shareholders should be examined. New mutual or local banks without shareholders should be given time to build up capital reserves and the regulator should welcome attempts by such institutions to find more instruments, such as non-dividend paying shares, that can absorb losses and provide banks with tier one capital.

## Creating a legal structure for local banks

The sale of the Trustee Savings Banks in 1986 was immensely detrimental to the health of the British banking market. The sale was able to occur because the banks were not safeguarded by a legal structure that enshrined their business model and ownership. It was not clear who owned the banks and what the trustees of the banks were permitted to do with them. This would be unthinkable in Germany or Switzerland where the goals and ownership of the Sparkassen and Cantonal banks are clearly laid out in statute.

The Government needs to create a legal framework that commits local banks to supporting their local economy. In the Trustee Savings Banks, the executives were constrained by trustees responsible for the bank's operations. However, a broader legal framework is required to constrain the actions of the trustees. This legal framework could be similar to that which outlines the duties of the trustees in a charity. The Charity Commission states that trustees must:

> Ensure that the charity does not breach any of the requirements or rules set out in its governing document and that it remains true to the charitable purpose and objects set out there.[130]

In much the same way a local bank would have to remain true to its objective of serving its local community and would be prohibited from doing anything that would jeopardise its ability to do so. The 'governing document' of a local bank would include the following objectives and limitations that the trustees or supervisory body would need to enforce:

1. **A local bank should have to generate profit by serving their local community**. It is often remarked that the Sparkassen pursue a 'dual bottom line' strategy so that generating profit does not override the need to serve the local community. Any local bank in the UK should be required to follow a similar approach.

2. **The supervisory body that oversees the actions of the bank should not be involved in commercial decisions**. The Sparkassen and Cantonal banks are successful because they are commercial institutions. The involvement of local government does not mean that money is used for party political purposes. Similarly the

Airdrie Savings Bank is successful because local businessmen who act as trustees do not abuse their position. A clear separation between oversight and the running of the bank is necessary for commercial success and legitimacy.

3. **Local banks should have no voting shareholders**. Local banks should have no shareholders in the traditional sense, nor would they be full mutuals because this would provide members with the opportunity to demutualise, as was the case with many British mutuals in the 1980s. Local banks should be safeguarded by statute but customers should be allowed to acquire non-voting shares, perhaps like the permanent interest bearing shares (PIBS) currently sold by building societies. Shares could be limited to customers and so shareholding would be restricted to the local area. The bank would thus have two sources of tier one capital: retained earnings and non-voting, permanent interest bearing shares.

4. **All lending decisions by the bank should be made at the local level by employees who know the local economy**. Local banks thrive because customers value their relationship with the branch of their local bank. Such relationships are built on the knowledge that is gained by branch staff having to take responsibility for their decisions on lending to local customers. If it is the case that a customer requires a loan that is too large for their local branch to provide, then it may be necessary for the central office of the local bank to make a decision on a loan. However, any decision made by the central office must be approved at branch level.

5. **The principle of geographic exclusivity should be enforced**. It is important for a local bank to be rooted in the local community and limiting its field of operations is the most effective way to ensure this. The exact area that a bank must restrict its operations to is something that would have to be decided by the bank based on its circumstances. A city could be an appropriate economic unit, so could a region.

6. **Local banks should have to adopt strict rules on mortgage lending**. Lending for property purposes by British banks grew dramatically between 2000 and 2010, while the level of businesses

lending was almost static. This is partly the result of banks adopting incredibly lax mortgage rules with the belief that rising house prices would offset the substantial risk. The Government and the FSA will impose stricter mortgage rules in 2013 but local banks should have to adopt even stricter rules. It is important that more banks in the UK lend to businesses and stricter mortgage rules are one way to encourage local banks to do this. This will not adversely affect consumers that wish to take out a mortgage, who can still approach other lenders. Local banks will not be prevented from offering mortgages but will be unable to build their business around mortgage lending.

Examining the current state of the mortgage market it is proposed that local banks should only be permitted to offer mortgages to customers that are able to put down a 25 per cent deposit based on the purchase price or valuation price of the property. Research carried out by Credit Choices, the independent consumer information company, indicated that 49.1 per cent of mortgages on the market require a deposit of 25 per cent or more, First Direct also estimated that the average deposit was 27 per cent.[131]

7. **The bank should not engage in proprietary trading**. Local banks should not use their own money to make investments to generate further income. Profits should be used to serve customers or bolster tier one capital.

8. **Local banks should not engage in investment banking activities**. Along similar lines to the demand by the Vickers Commission, local banks should not engage in investment banking activities such as underwriting, trading, mergers and acquisitions, sales of derivatives and other products for hedging risk and the other activities that are carried out by the investment banking arms of Britain's universal banks. Local banks should be able to serve large, non-financial corporate clients with loans and other retail services, but should not be able to offer investment banking services or products to these clients.

9. **Each local bank should have to publish a simple, standardised breakdown of their balance sheet, clearly outlining what assets**

**it holds and what liabilities it is answerable for.** This will help regulators but also allow customers to examine what their local bank is investing in. Transparency and accountability will help consumers make informed choices and other banks should be encouraged to do the same.

Trustees, or those charged with overseeing the operations of the bank, should be legally required to ensure that these objectives and limitations are adhered to.

Not only would a specific legal structure ensure that local banks served their communities but it would also make it easier for regulators to assess and approve banks. A standardised constitution would allow the FSA or FCA to approve banks that adhered to the pre-approved legal structure and accompanying regulations.

## *Encouraging the growth of local banks*

Once a clear legal framework governing local banks is in place, its use should be encouraged. At present, it is very difficult to set up a bank because of the regulatory hurdles. It is also very difficult to set up a bank because of the complexity of the task and the cost.

Estimates of those with experience of setting up new banks put start-up costs at approximately £110 million. This includes £40 million for the systems, infrastructure and personnel, and £70 million in reserves and working capital. Start-up costs are obviously dependent on the size of the bank planned and some analysts put a figure of £10 million on the cost of the infrastructure, systems and personnel. Nevertheless, it is remarkable how much cheaper it is to set up a bank in America. In America prospective banks look to generate start-up investment of approximately $20 million (£13 million), including $2 million (£1.3 million) for the infrastructure and systems and $15-$20 million (£9.8 million - £13 million) for working capital and reserves.

This discrepancy is partly the result of the cost of banking technology. In America, there are lots of companies that provide off-the-shelf banking software at a significantly lower cost than UK providers, which are more accustomed to handling the technology requirements of Britain's large firms. Britain needs to develop a market for low-cost off-the-shelf banking software. Such software could reduce the start-up costs for new banks to those seen in America.

Alongside the technology costs and the regulatory hurdles there are also legal and technical requirements for new banks. Banks must comply with money laundering regulations, accounting standards have to be adhered to, and various security and health and safety measures must be put in place, along with all other general business regulations. The Government could provide this information, in a similar way that the Charity Commission provides a step-by-step guide to setting up a charity, to prospective banks and, in particular, those who wished to set up a local bank for the benefit of their community. The Government could provide examples of the necessary paper work, recommend IT suppliers and explain the duties of the bank's executives and trustees. Such action is necessary so that people can be made aware of the opportunities for creating new local banks.

As well as allowing and encouraging private individuals or organisations to create local banks, the Government, bearing in mind the success of such institutions in Switzerland and Germany, should support any local authority that wished to set up a local bank.

## *Local authorities and local banks*

In November 2011, the Localism Act became law. It provides local authorities with a 'general power of competence' which gives them the ability to 'act in the interest of their communities and in their own financial interest to generate efficiencies and secure value for money outcomes'. Supporters of the law welcome the fact that it gives local authorities the power to set up a business for the benefit of their local community, including a bank. It is perhaps less well-known that local authorities already had the power to accept deposits and make loans. The Financial Markets and Services Act 2000 (Exemption) Order 2001 freed local authorities from being regulated by the FSA and achieving FSA approval when making loans and accepting deposits. The upshot of both the Localism Act and the exemption in the Financial Markets and Services Act is that local authorities can readily establish local banks.

One advantage of local authority involvement is that they have sufficient resources to begin taking deposits and making loans in a relatively short amount of time. They do not require FSA approval, which can be a protracted process, and many already possess the capital to meet the necessary reserve requirements. Local authorities are also in a good position to appreciate the credit needs of their local community.

It is understandable that some people are wary of government involvement in banking and fear that money will be used to support favoured businesses or political projects. However, the German and Swiss examples illustrate how government can act as a responsible trustee without any involvement in the commercial operations of the bank. A suitable model for British local banks has been outlined above and the Government could ensure local authorities adopt it, or one like it, when establishing a local bank. The Government should make it very clear that any local authority can set up a bank if they feel that there is an unmet demand for such a service in their area.

Another concern is that a local authority bank would unfairly compete with private banks. Leaving aside the issue that Britain's dominant commercial banks have almost oligopolic control over the market at present, it is already clear that commercial banks benefit significantly from implicit Government backing. Research carried out by the New Economics Foundation using work by Andrew Haldane, Executive Director of Financial Stability at the Bank of England, estimated that Barclays, Lloyds, HSBC, RBS and Nationwide receive an annual subsidy of approximately £30 billion through reduced funding costs, the result of their *de facto* public guarantee.[132] This figure does not include the money that banks have generated through their involvement in quantitative easing where the Bank of England has bought government bonds off banks, or through banks, to increase the money supply. This has allowed banks to earn money on commission when trading the bonds as well as generate income by selling the bonds to the Bank of England at a higher price than they bought them for.[133] There is little chance that these subsidies will decrease in the future; banks now enjoy an almost explicit guarantee after the Government saved a number of large banks during the crisis and further rounds of quantitative easing are likely in the future. Despite this, those critical of the idea of local authorities setting up local banks may voice concerns about unfair competition with smaller banks. Such fears are overblown. Local authority banks would be run as commercial enterprises and would have to compete as such. Furthermore, local authorities would welcome competition that improved outcomes for their constituents. Market share would not be a priority, as it is with commercial banks.

The Government would not have to force local authorities to open banks. The evidence is that there are many enterprising local authorities that would wish to do so. The 'Bank of Essex' and the proposed reopening of the Birmingham Municipal Bank indicates the real interest in local banking of local authorities that are aware of the lack of supportive financial institutions in their communities.[134] Sadly both ideas failed because neither actually created, nor planned to create, a local bank, both schemes were short-term funds run alongside commercial lenders. As well as local authorities, there are now 16 directly elected mayors in the UK and future referendums in other localities could increase this number. The Government has encouraged the spread of local mayors as a way to devolve more decision-making power. Local mayors, elected with a mandate to address problems in their community, may feel that a local bank is a good way to support their local economy.

There is a strong case for using public money to help set up local banks in areas where businesses are being starved of credit. The challenge for the Government will be to use public money wisely to support the most worthwhile projects. One way in which the Government could demonstrate its support for local banks without spending significant amounts of public money would be to invite bids by local authorities or mayors. The best bids, both in terms of the quality of the proposal and the needs of the community, should be awarded grants or low-interest loans to fund the creation of local banks.

The Government is likely to argue that there is little or no public funding for this project. However, the sums required are minimal. Banks could be set up with as little as £20 million. The Regional Growth Fund (RGF) aims to help areas of the country that are likely to suffer most from the public spending cuts due to a lack of private-sector employment. Many such areas suffer from a lack of finance. The RGF has £2.4 billion to disburse and plans to do so through rounds of bidding. Nevertheless it is widely expected that there will be a significant sum of money left over after the bidding rounds. Bids may be successful but, on closer scrutiny, be unworkable and it is highly unlikely that money will be granted to all successful projects. This is not surprising given the nature of investment and the uncertainties involved.

It is proposed that the Government should use excess funds from the RGF to support the creation of local banks, by local authorities or mayors, through a competitive tendering process. If the Government does not wish to use the RGF, it should consider another source of funding. Starting four local banks would cost less than £100 million, a minuscule amount when one considers the money disbursed by other Government initiatives.

## Local banks and other financial institutions

The success of local banks in serving local businesses has been the focus of this report, however local banks in Germany, Switzerland and the UK also help tackle financial exclusion. The Sparkassen must open a bank account for any customer who wants one and the group keeps branches open in areas that the commercial banks view as unprofitable.[135] The Cantonal banks are bound by a similar legal requirement to serve local customers regardless of their wealth, and the Trustee Savings Banks were the banks for small savers for a century and a half until they were privatised.

Nevertheless, financial exclusion is about more than just access to finance and the ability to open a bank account. In this country, financial exclusion is often addressed by credit unions or Community Development Finance Institutions (CDFIs).

Since January 2012 credit unions have been able to compete directly with banks. This is the result of a Legislative Reform Order passed by Parliament which altered the 1979 Credit Unions Act. The Order allows credit unions to serve a wider range of individuals and businesses and pay interest on savings. The Government has set up a £73 million fund to help credit unions make use of their new powers.

To help credit unions expand their operations and provide a realistic alternative to the commercial banks, the Government should ensure that this money is used to invest in banking software that can allow credit unions to work together to create a strong sector. Credit unions should use the public funding to buy off-the-shelf banking software from an established provider. Software such as the Kasasa system offered by the American company BankVue would allow credit unions to use a common infrastructure so that customers could be served by many different unions.

Credit unions can provide an effective alternative to the commercial banks for businesses and individuals if they can be encouraged to make the full use of their new powers. However, this should not come at the expense of addressing financial exclusion which is a particular strength of the credit unions and the CDFIs.

CDFIs were officially recognised in the 1990s as a way in which individuals on low-income or with little access to the commercial banks could access financial services. CDFIs do not take deposits but offer loans, and some provide advisory services. Each CDFI is different and often offer different services and products including business loans, personal loans and housing loans. In 2010, the average loan from a CDFI to a micro-business was £10,007 although CDFIs lent between £500 and upwards of £60,000. In March 2010, when the latest data was published by the Community Development Finance Association (CDFA), 66 CDFIs across the UK had a combined loan portfolio of £531 million with a further £260 million available to lend.[136]

CDFIs provide an important service that goes beyond the loans that they make to micro-businesses and SMEs. Many CDFIs also provide advice, helping people manage their finances better, and offer an alternative to loan sharks when people run into financial difficulty. The difficulty faced by the majority of CDFIs is that they are not financially self-sustaining. On average, earned income accounted for only 40 per cent of the funding requirements of the CDFI sector in 2010.[137] The risk is that any push to make CDFIs self-sustaining could imperil the valuable social work the sector does by forcing them to focus on wealthier clients.[138] This is an issue that cannot be addressed in this publication, however it does indicate how the Government needs to consider other financial issues and examine how financial institutions can work together to address them. Ensuring that businesses have access to finance and tackling financial exclusion are interrelated. Local banks can help address the first issue and may be able to mitigate the second, but the Government should also examine how local banks can work with other institutions.

The suggestions made in this report will not have the intended effect if they are implemented in isolation. Reducing the barriers to entry for prospective banks is a means to an end, the end being a more effective financial sector that serves local economies. Only by encouraging the development of local banks will the Government help bring about real reform of the British banking market.

# *Notes*

**Preface**
1. Clarke, S. L., *German savings banks and Swiss Cantonal banks, lessons for the UK*, Civitas, December 2010.

**1. The British banking market**
2. Centre for the Study of Financial Innovation, *Views on Vickers: responses to the ICB report*, November 2011.
3. Cruikshank, D., Competition *in UK Banking: A Report to the Chancellor of the Exchequer*, March 2000.
4. House of Commons Treasury Select Committee, *Competition and choice in retail banking Ninth Report of Session 2010–11*, March 2011, p. 15.
5. Fraser, S., *Small Firms in the Credit Crisis: Evidence from the UK Survey of SME Finances*, Centre for Small and Medium-Sized Enterprises, Warwick Business School, University of Warwick, 2009, p. 13.
6. *Competition and choice in retail banking Ninth Report of Session 2010–11*.
7. *Competition and choice in retail banking Ninth Report of Session 2010–11*.
8. Fraser, *Small Firms in the Credit Crisis: Evidence from the UK Survey of SME Finances*, p. 5.
9. Fast growing businesses are businesses born before 2003 that experienced 72.8 per cent or more growth in employment between 2005 and 2008.
10. Bank of England, *Trends in Lending*, October 2011, p. 4.
11. *Trends in Lending*, p. 7.
12. The indicative median interest rate is calculated by the Bank of England by assessing the price of SME facilities, above the base rate, offered by four major lenders (Barclays, HSBC, Lloyds Banking Group and Royal Bank of Scotland)
13. *Trends in Lending*, p. 8.
14. Bank of England, *Credit Conditions Survey, Survey Results Q3 2011*, September 2011, p. 16.
15. Kay, J., visiting Professor of Economics at the London School of Economics in *Views on Vickers: Responses to the ICB Report*, 2011, p. 42.
16. 'Cable tells banks to increase lending to small firms', *BBC News*, 23 May 2011.
17. 'David Cameron admits difficulties in getting banks to lend more', *The Guardian*, 1 November 2010.
18. 'MPC's Adam Posen calls on Government to set up state bank to help small businesses', *The Telegraph*, 14 September 2011.
19. 'Best banks for customer service revealed: First Direct top, Santander bottom in Which? Poll', *Customer Service Network*, 29 September 2011.
20. 'The top five banks for customer service', *Thisismoney.co.uk*, 1 October 2010.
21. Coyle, D., in *Views on Vickers: Responses to the ICB Report*, 2011 p. 27.

[22] 'One in four mobile internet users using mobile banking', *Antenna*, 30 June 2011. The 14 banks were: HSBC, First Direct, RBS, Natwest, Barclays, Nationwide, Lloyds TSB, Santander, Halifax, Standard Chartered, Bank of Scotland, Metro Bank, Northern Rock, and Cheltenham and Gloucester. The survey only looked for dedicated apps and mobile websites and did not take into account text alert services or downloadable web icons with quick access to mobile banking sites, which some of the above did offer. The results are based on banks' mobile offerings as of 17th June 2011.

[23] 'Banks have closed 434 branches in three years', *The Telegraph*, 3 April 2010.

## 2. Swiss Cantonal banks

[24] The Association of Swiss Cantonal Banks, *The Cantonal Banks A Swiss Banking Group*, 2009, p. 4.

[25] Swiss National Bank, *Banks in Switzerland 2010*, 2011.

[26] Margelisch, C., Speech for Swiss Bankers Association, *Banking Barometer, too-big-to-fail and macroprudential supervision*, 5 September 2011, p. 2. Accessed at: http://www.swissbanking.org/en/20110905-5720-dok-refmkcma_d-tsu_final.pdf

[27] Calculations based on the assumption that 90 per cent of the lending of the Cantonal banks is domestic, as indicated by the Association of Swiss Cantonal Banks. Figures taken from the Swiss National Bank, *Monthly Bulletin of Banking Statistics*, October 2011, p. 97.

[28] Neuberger, D., Pedergnana, M. & Räthke-Döppner, S., 'Concentration of Banking Relationships in Switzerland: The Result of Firm Structure or Banking Market Structure?' *Journal of Financial Services Research* 33, (2), 2008, pp. 101-126.

[29] *The Cantonal Banks A Swiss Banking Group*, p. 4

[30] Those with 50 – 249 employees.

[31] Those with 10 – 49 employees.

[32] Those with 1 – 9 employees.

[33] Neuberger, D. & Schacht, C., 'The Number of Bank Relationships of SMEs: A Disaggregated Analysis for the Swiss Loan Market', *Economic Notes* 35, (3), 2007, pp. 319 – 353.

[34] The Association of Swiss Cantonal Banks, *The balance sheets and profit & loss accounts of the Cantonal Banks as of 30.06.2011*, 2011

[35] 'Banque Cantonale du Jura SA', *ft.com/marketsdata*, Data from 24 Jun 2011 - 31 Dec 2011

[36] *The balance sheets and profit & loss accounts of the Cantonal Banks as of 30.06.2011*

[37] Article 98 Clause 1 of the Federal Constitution of the Swiss Confederation of 18 April 1999 (Status as of 1 January 2011)

[38] Article 3a of the Swiss Federal Law on Banks and Savings Banks of 8 November 1934 (status as of 1 January 2009)

[39] Neher, S., 'Distribution of the shareholder base of Swiss cantonal banks', *Financial Markets and Portfolio Management* 21, (4), 2007, pp. 471-485.

[40] 21 of the Cantonal banks have a Cantonal guarantee and of these, 14 have to pay for it.
[41] Article 12A(3) of the Law on Banque cantonale de Genève of June 24 1993.
[42] Law on Banque cantonale de Genève of June 24 1993.
[43] Translation from the German in 'Distribution of the shareholder base of Swiss cantonal banks'.
[44] Neher, 'Distribution of the shareholder base of Swiss cantonal banks'.
[45] Neher, 'Distribution of the shareholder base of Swiss cantonal banks'.
[46] 'UBS revises 2008 losses higher', *The Guardian*, 11 March 2009.
[47] *Monthly Bulletin of Banking Statistics September 2011*, pg. 96
[48] The Swiss Central Bank groups banks together and gives the profits and the losses for the banks in the group. The two big banks managed to post both a profit and a loss for 2007 because Credit Suisse posted a profit while UBS posted a loss. The same applies for the cantonal banks in 2008, when some posted a loss but the majority posted a profit.

## 3. The German Sparkassen

[49] Ayadi, R., Schmidt, R.H., Valverde, S.C., Arbak, E. & Fernandez, F.R., *Investigating Diversity in the Banking Sector in Europe: The Performance and Role of Savings Banks*, Centre for European Policy Studies, 2009.
[50] According to evidence from *Small Firms in the Credit Crisis: Evidence from the UK Survey of SME Finances*, and KEW/KfW, *Grundungspanel*, 2009.
[51] The Länder are the German states. Historically each land had its own Landesbank, although there are now only 7 Landesbanken for the 16 Länder due to mergers.
[52] The section of the German Banking Act which describes which institutions can obtain a banking licence.
[53] Part 3, Division 2, Section 40 of the Banking Act of the Federal Republic of Germany (Kreditwesengesetz, KWG), Translation by Deutsche Bundesbank.
[54] Brunner, A. D., *Germany's Three-Pillar banking System: Cross-country Perspectives in Europe*, 2004.
[55] Thuringia Savings Bank Act of 19 July 1994 (Thüringer Sparkassengesetz (ThürSpKG) Vom 19. Juli 1994).
[56] Schmidt, A. G., & Selbherr, G., 'Tasks, Organization and Economic Benefits of the German Guarantee Banks', *Journal for SME Development* 11, 2009, pp. 85-126.
[57] Schmidt & Selbherr, 'Tasks, Organization and Economic Benefits of the German Guarantee Banks'.
[58] 'Lending to SMEs under EFG scheme falls to record low', *SMEWEB*, 22 December 2011.
[59] Schmidt, A. G. & Elkan, M. V., *Macroeconomic benefits of the German Guarantee Banks under the framework conditions of the global financial and economic crisis*, Institut für Mittelstandsökonomie an der Universität Trier, 2010 and Schmidt, A. G. & Elkan, M. V., *Macroeconomic benefits of the German Guarantee Banks*, Institut für Mittelstandsökonomie an der Universität Trier, 2006.

[60] The Association of German Guarantee Banks, *The German Guarantee Banks 2009*, 2010 (Der Verband Deutscher Bürgschaftsbankendie, *Die Deutschen Bürgschaftsbanken 2009*, 2010).
[61] Schmidt & Elkan, *Macroeconomic benefits of the German Guarantee Banks under the framework conditions of the global financial and economic crisis*.
[62] Schmidt & Elkan, *Macroeconomic benefits of the German Guarantee Banks*.
[63] *The German Guarantee Banks 2009*.
[64] Deutsche Bundesbank, *Lending to domestic enterprises and self-employed persons*, 2011.
[65] The World Bank.
[66] Hüfner, F., 'The German Banking System: Lessons from the Financial Crisis', *OECD Economics Department Working Papers*, No. 788, OECD Publishing, 2010, p. 14.

**4. Trustee Savings Banks**

[67] Horne, H. O., *A History of Savings Banks*, 1947, p. 50.
[68] Horne, *A History of Savings Banks*, p. 91.
[69] Horne, *A History of Savings Banks*, pp. 80 -81.
[70] Horne, *A History of Savings Banks*, p. 81.
[71] Horne, *A History of Savings Banks*, p. 77.
[72] Horne, *A History of Savings Banks*, p. 333.
[73] Horne, *A History of Savings Banks*, p. 351.
[74] *The Cantonal Banks, A Swiss Banking Group*.
[75] Marshall, I., TSB Group Central Executive, 'Strategic Issues for the Trustee Savings Banks', *Long Range Planning* 18, (4), 1985, pp. 39-43.
[76] Horne, *A History of Savings Banks*, p. 389.
[77] Maixé-Altés, J. C., 'Enterprise and philanthropy: the dilemma of Scottish savings banks in the late nineteenth century', *Accounting, Business & Financial History* 19, (1), 2009, pp. 39-59.
[78] Maixé-Altés, 'Enterprise and philanthropy: the dilemma of Scottish savings banks in the late nineteenth century'.
[79] Horne, *A History of Savings Banks*, p. 316.
[80] I have chosen to break with the series in 1913 because the activities of the SIDs were severely disrupted by the First World War.
[81] I have chosen to end the series in 1939 because the activities of the SIDs were severely disrupted by the Second World War.
[82] 'TSB "could be worth £1 bn"', *The Financial Times*, 18 January 1984
[83] Sampson, A., 'How not to privatise', *Economic Affairs* 7, (3), 1987, pp. 28-30.
[84] 'But whose is it to give away?', *The Guardian*, 5 August 1986
[85] For the former see: Sampson, 'How not to privatise'. For the latter see: Davidmann, M., *The Trustee Savings Bank Give-Away*, 1996. Accessed at: http://www.solhaam.org/articles/tsb.html
[86] Percival, M., 'The banks that like to litigate', *Modern Law Review* 50, (2), March 1987, pp. 231-240.

[87] Percival, 'The banks that like to litigate'.
[88] 'Flotation of TSB ignores ruling', *The Guardian*, 5 August 1986
[89] 'Heavy prospectus demand for Trustee Savings Bank', *The Financial Times*, 16 September 1986
[90] TSB shares were paid for in instalments, and so when the first shares were sold individuals were able to purchase half shares with the understanding that they would purchase full shares at a later date.
[91] ' TSB shares open at 100p', *The Financial Times*, 11 October 1986
[92] Graham, C., 'Privatization – The United Kingdom Experience', *Brooklyn Journal of International Law*, 1995-1996, pp. 185-213.
[93] 'Co-op set to become big banker', *BBC Robert Peston*, 14 December 2011.

## 5. Localised banking today: The Airdrie Savings Bank and Handelsbanken

[94] Airdrie Savings Bank, *Annual Report and Accounts 2010*, 2011.
[95] 'Airdrie Savings Bank Boring, stolid, small and safe, How one bank stuck to its last and prospered', *The Economist*, 13 November 2008.
[96] *Annual Report and Accounts 2010*, p. 9.
[97] *Annual Report and Accounts 2010*, p. 9.
[98] 'Boss and staff at Airdrie Savings Bank took pay cut', *Herald Scotland*, 25 January 2011.
[99] Clause I of the Savings Bank (Scotland) Act 1819
[100] 'Airdrie Savings Bank's alternative vision', *Scotsman.com*, 25 August 2010
[101] *Annual Report and Accounts 2010*, p. 10.
[102] 'Airdrie Savings Bank Boring, stolid, small and safe, How one bank stuck to its last and prospered', *The Economist*.
[103] *Annual Report and Accounts 2010*, p. 20.
[104] 'Airdrie Savings Bank Boring, stolid, small and safe, How one bank stuck to its last and prospered', *The Economist*.
[105] Kroner, N., *A Blueprint for Better Banking, Svenska Handelsbanken and a proven model for more stable and profitable banking*, 2009, p. 105.
[106] Handelsbanken, *Factbook 2011 Q3*, 2011.
[107] *Factbook 2010 Q4*.
KPMG, *UK Banks: Performance Benchmarking Report Full Year Results 2010*, March 2011, RBS and Lloyds did not disclose return on equity.
[108] *Factbook 2009 Q1, 2010 Q1, 2011 Q3*.
[109] *Factbook 2010 Q4*.
[110] 'Co-op set to become big banker', *BBC Robert Peston*.

## 6. The barriers to British local banks

[111] Henry, A., Chairman, Chief Executive and principle shareholder of Arbuthnot Banking Group & Turrell, A., Vice-Chairman of Arbuthnot Securities in *Views on Vickers: Responses to the ICB Report*, p. 11.

[112] Osborne, G., Chancellor of the Exchequer, giving evidence to the Treasury Select Committee on the Independent Commission on Banking: Final Report, 11 January 2012.
[113] Financial Services Authority, *Applying for authorisation*, p. 6.
[114] Evidence provided by those that have been through the application process. The FSA's preference for banks with a 'high-street' presence is also clear in the way it sets liquidity penalties for banks that offer online-only accounts.
[115] Kay, J., visiting Professor of Economics at the London School of Economics, giving evidence to the Treasury Select Committee as part of the Independent Commission on Banking: Final Report, 18 October 2011
[116] Hansard, Column 512, 24 Nov 2011.
[117] 'Dave vs the banking giants – Channel 4 commissions new series', *Channel 4 Press*, August 11 2011.
[118] A set of agreements drawn up in the Swiss city of Basel
[119] Financial Services Authority, *Strengthening liquidity standards*, October 2009, p. 45.
[120] *Strengthening liquidity standards*, p. 45.
[121] Deloitte, *Building Society Update 7*, Spring 2011.
[122] Rhodes, C., Group Product & Marketing Director of Nationwide, giving evidence to the Treasury Select Committee as part of the Independent Commission on Banking: Final Report, 26 October 2011.
[123] Rhodes, C., giving evidence to the Treasury Select Committee as part of the Independent Commission on Banking: Final Report.
[124] 'Our banks can stay open – and save £1bn', *The Sunday Telegraph*, September 4 2011
[125] Henry Angest & Atholl Turrell, in *Views on Vickers: Responses to the ICB Report*, p. 11.
[126] *Building Society Update*, p.4.
[127] 'Reaction to Basel III rules for banks', *The Telegraph*, September 13 2010.
[128] 'Reaction to Basel III rules for banks', *The Telegraph*.
[129] Potter, P., former Deputy Chairman of Investec Bank UK in *Views on Vickers: Responses to the ICB Report*, p. 54.

## 7. Conclusion: British local banks

[130] Charity Commission, *The Essential Trustee: What you need to know*, February 2008.
[131] 'How big a deposit do I need to get a mortgage in 2011?', *Credit Choices*, 10 March 2011. 'Homebuyers now paying higher deposit than ever, research finds', *The Guardian*, 17 September 2011.
[132] Greenham, T., Simms, A., Prieg, L. & Potts, R., *Feather-bedding Financial Services Are British banks getting hidden subsidies?*, New Economics Foundation, February 2011.
[133] Greenham, Simms, Prieg & Potts, *Feather-bedding Financial Services Are British banks getting hidden subsidies?*.

## NOTES

[134] 'Santander is backing Bank of Essex', *ThisisMoney.co.uk*, March 22 2009. 'Birmingham Municipal Bank could reopen, hints Mike Whitby', *Birmingham Post*, December 4 2008.

[135] Ayadi, Schmidt, Valverde, Arbak & Fernandez, *Investigating Diversity in the Banking Sector in Europe: The Performance and Role of Savings Banks*.

[136] CDFA, *Inside Out 2010 The State of Community Development Finance*, December 2010

[137] *Inside Out 2010 The State of Community Development Finance*.

[138] Thiel, V. & Nissan, S., UK *CDFIs – From Surviving to Thriving, realising the potential of community development finance*, New Economics Foundation, 2008.